MARVEL

ULTIMATE SPIDER-MAN

vs

THE SINISTER 6

MARVEL UNIVERSE ULTIMATE SPIDER-MAN VS. THE SINISTER SIX VOL. 1. Contains material originally published in magazine form as MARVEL UNIVERSE ULTIMATE SPIDER-MAN VS. THE SINISTER SIX #1-4. First printing 2017. ISBN# 978-1-302-90258-2. Published by MARVEL WORLDWIDE, INC., a subsidiary of MARVEL ENTERTAINMENT, LLC. OFFICE OF PUBLICATION: 135 West 50th Street, New York, NY 10020. Copyright © 2017 MARVEL No similarity between any of the names, characters, persons, and/or institutions in this magazine with those of any living or dead person or institution is intended, and any such similarity which may exist is purely coincidental. **Printed in the U.S.A.** ALAN FINE, President, Marvel Entertainment; DAN BUCKLEY, President, TV, Publishing & Brand Management; JOE QUESADA, Chief Creative Officer; TOM BREVOORT, SVP of Publishing; DAVID BOGART, SVP of Business Affairs & Operations, Publishing & Partnership; C.B. CEBULSKI, VP of Brand Management & Development, Asia; DAVID GABRIEL, SVP of Sales & Marketing, Publishing; JEFF YOUNGQUIST, VP of Production & Special Projects; DAN CARR, Executive Director of Publishing Technology; ALEX MORALES, Director of Publishing Operations; SUSAN CRESPI, Production Manager; STAN LEE, Chairman Emeritus. For information regarding advertising in Marvel Comics or on Marvel.com, please contact Vit DeBellis, Integrated Sales Manager, at vdebellis@marvel.com. For Marvel subscription inquiries, please call 888-511-5480. **Manufactured between 11/11/2016 and 12/19/2016 by SHERIDAN, CHELSEA, MI, USA.**

10 9 8 7 6 5 4 3 2 1

MARVEL
ULTIMATE SPIDER-MAN VS THE SINISTER 6

BASED ON THE TV SERIES WRITTEN BY
KEVIN BURKE & CHRIS "DOC" WYATT AND JACOB SEMAHN

DIRECTED BY
YOUNG KI YOON, JAE WOO KIM AND ROY BURDINE

ANIMATION PRODUCED BY
MARVEL ANIMATION STUDIOS WITH **FILM ROMAN**

ADAPTED BY
JOE CARAMAGNA

SPECIAL THANKS TO
HANNAH MCDONALD & PRODUCT FACTORY

EDITORS
CHRISTINA HARRINGTON WITH MARK BASSO

SENIOR EDITOR
MARK PANICCIA

SPIDER-MAN CREATED BY **STAN LEE & STEVE DITKO**

Collection Editor: **Jennifer Grünwald**
Associate Managing Editor: **Kateri Woody**
Associate Editor: **Sarah Brunstad**
Editor, Special Projects: **Mark D. Beazley**
VP Production & Special Projects: **Jeff Youngquist**
SVP Print, Sales & Marketing: **David Gabriel**
Head of Marvel Television: **Jeph Loeb**

Editor In Chief: **Axel Alonso**
Chief Creative Officer: **Joe Quesada**
Publisher: **Dan Buckley**
Executive Producer: **Alan Fine**

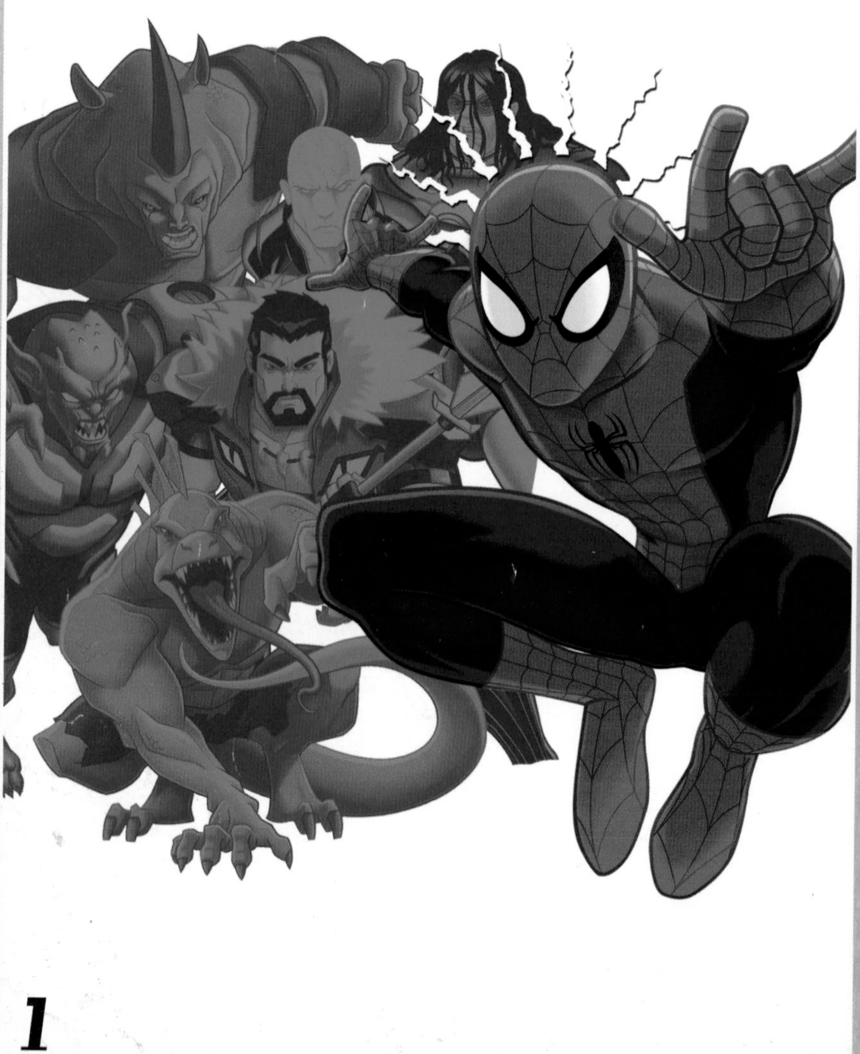

1

While attending a radiology demonstration, high school student Peter Parker was bitten by a radioactive spider and gained the spider's powers! Now he is training with the superspy organization called S.H.I.E.L.D. to become the...

MARVEL

ULTIMATE SPIDER-MAN VS THE SINISTER 6

The GOBLIN? Defeated. CONTEST OF CHAMPIONS? Nailed it. Aunt May knows all about Peter Parker's double life and is totally cool with it, and Peter's best friend Harry is getting along with his reformed dad, Norman. Yep! It seems like everything is coming up Spidey these days!

If only it would stay that way.

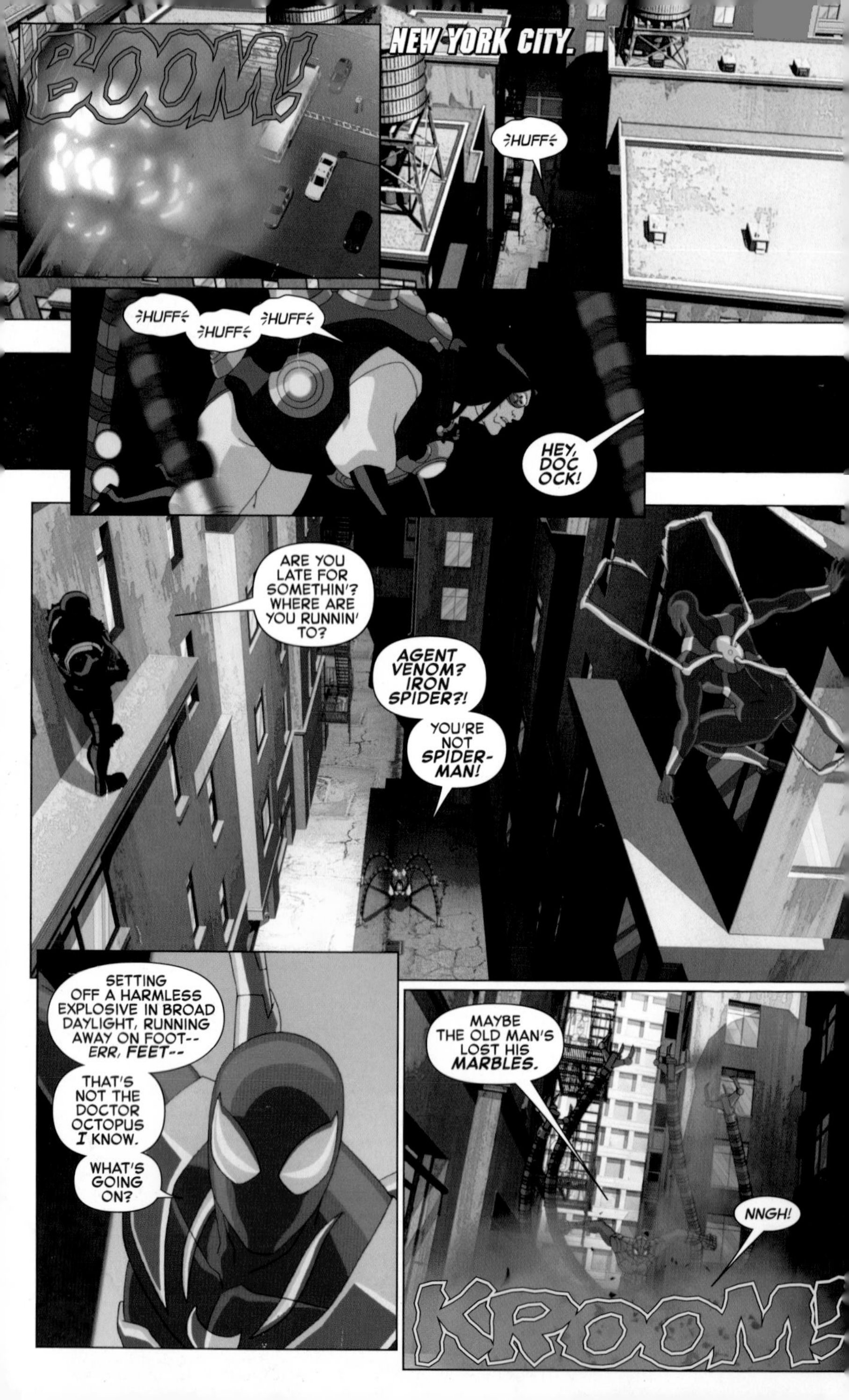
BOOM!
NEW YORK CITY.
HUFF
HUFF
HUFF
HUFF
HEY, DOC OCK!
ARE YOU LATE FOR SOMETHIN'? WHERE ARE YOU RUNNIN' TO?
AGENT VENOM? IRON SPIDER?!
YOU'RE NOT SPIDER-MAN!
SETTING OFF A HARMLESS EXPLOSIVE IN BROAD DAYLIGHT, RUNNING AWAY ON FOOT-- ERR, FEET--
THAT'S NOT THE DOCTOR OCTOPUS I KNOW.
WHAT'S GOING ON?
MAYBE THE OLD MAN'S LOST HIS MARBLES.
NNGH!
KROOM!

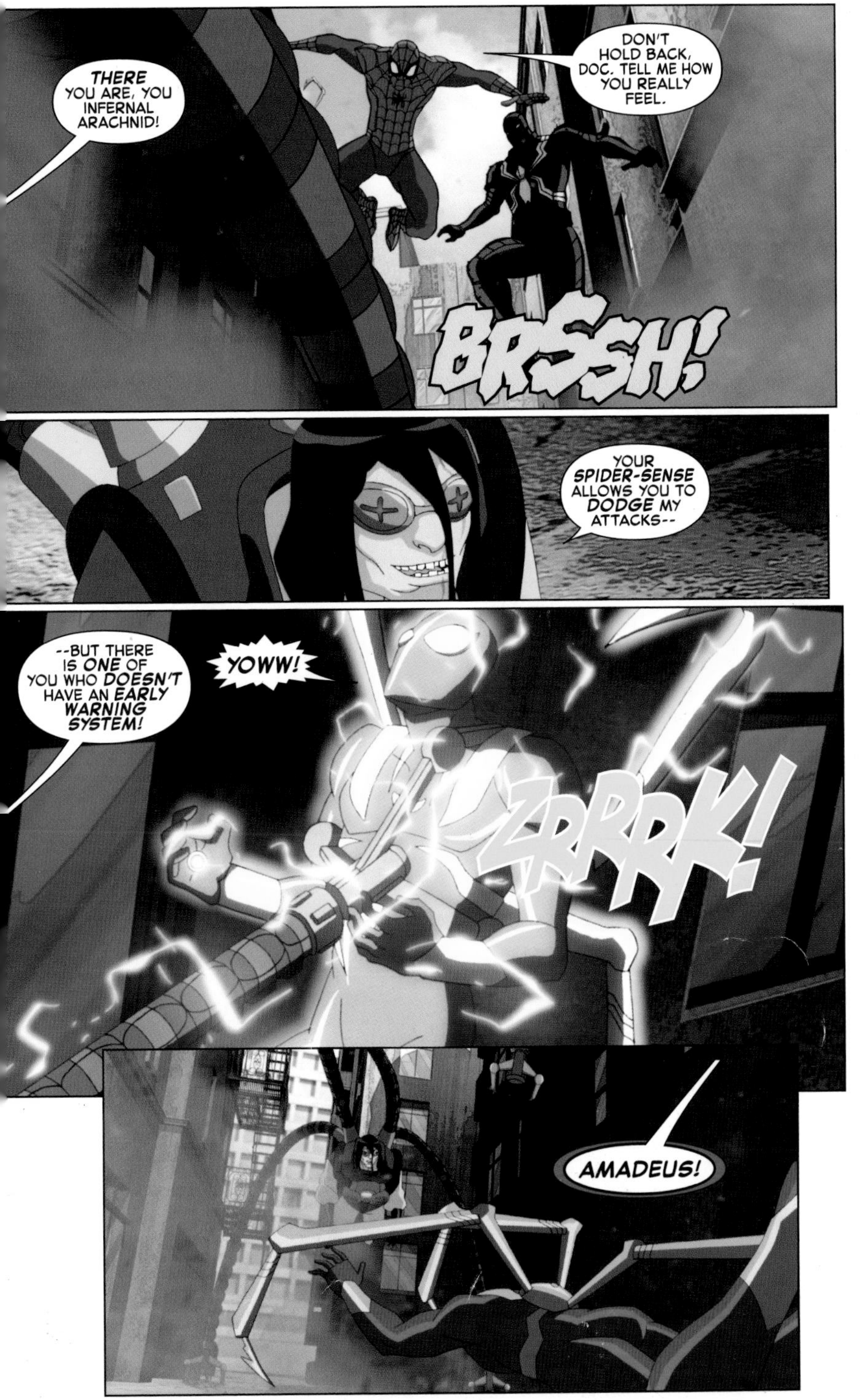
THERE YOU ARE, YOU INFERNAL ARACHNID!
DON'T HOLD BACK, DOC. TELL ME HOW YOU REALLY FEEL.
BRSSH!
YOUR SPIDER-SENSE ALLOWS YOU TO DODGE MY ATTACKS--
--BUT THERE IS ONE OF YOU WHO DOESN'T HAVE AN EARLY WARNING SYSTEM!
YOWW!
ZRRRK!
AMADEUS!

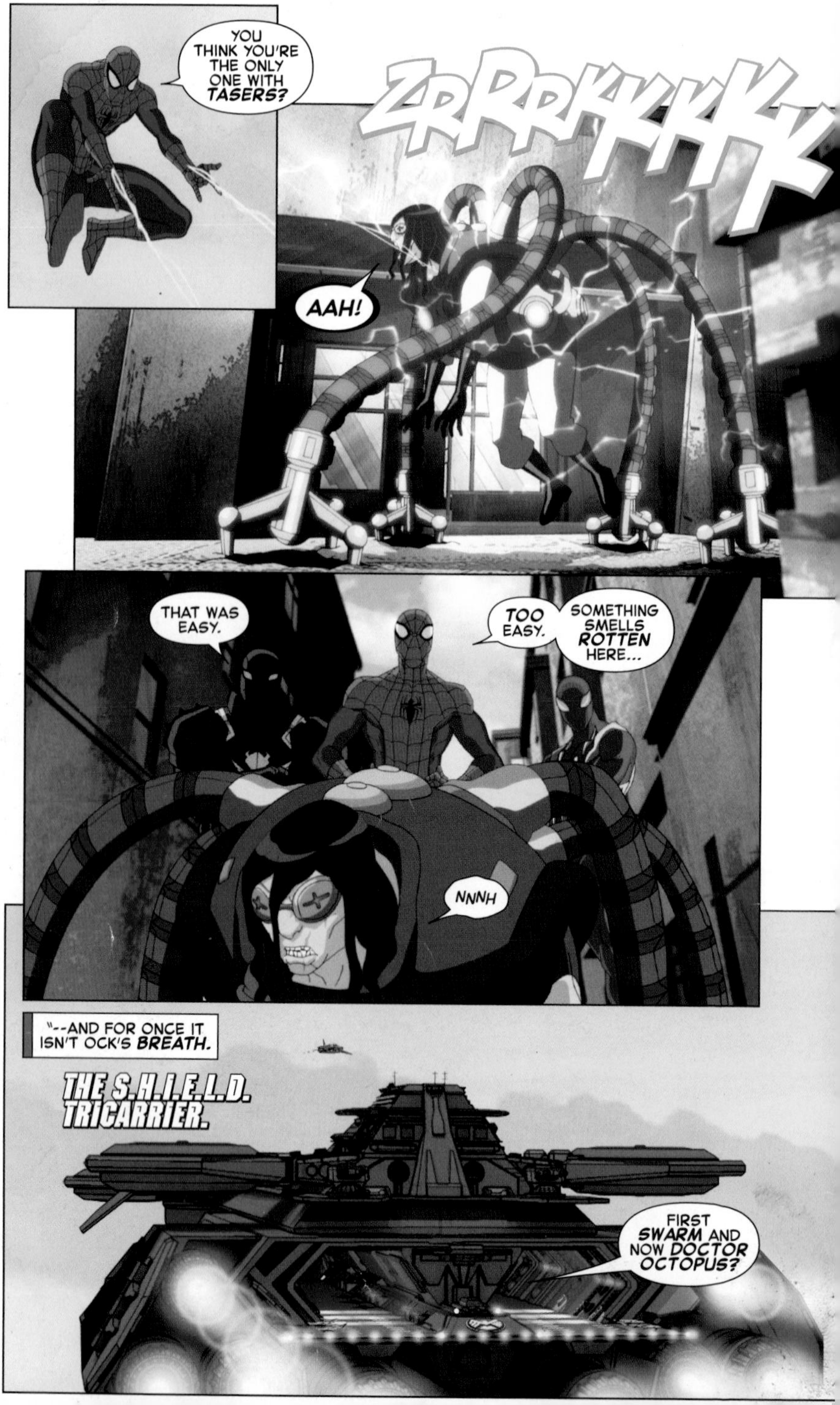
YOU THINK YOU'RE THE ONLY ONE WITH TASERS?
ZRRRKKKKK
AAH!
THAT WAS EASY.
TOO EASY.
SOMETHING SMELLS ROTTEN HERE...
NNNH
"--AND FOR ONCE IT ISN'T OCK'S BREATH.
THE S.H.I.E.L.D. TRICARRIER.
FIRST SWARM AND NOW DOCTOR OCTOPUS?

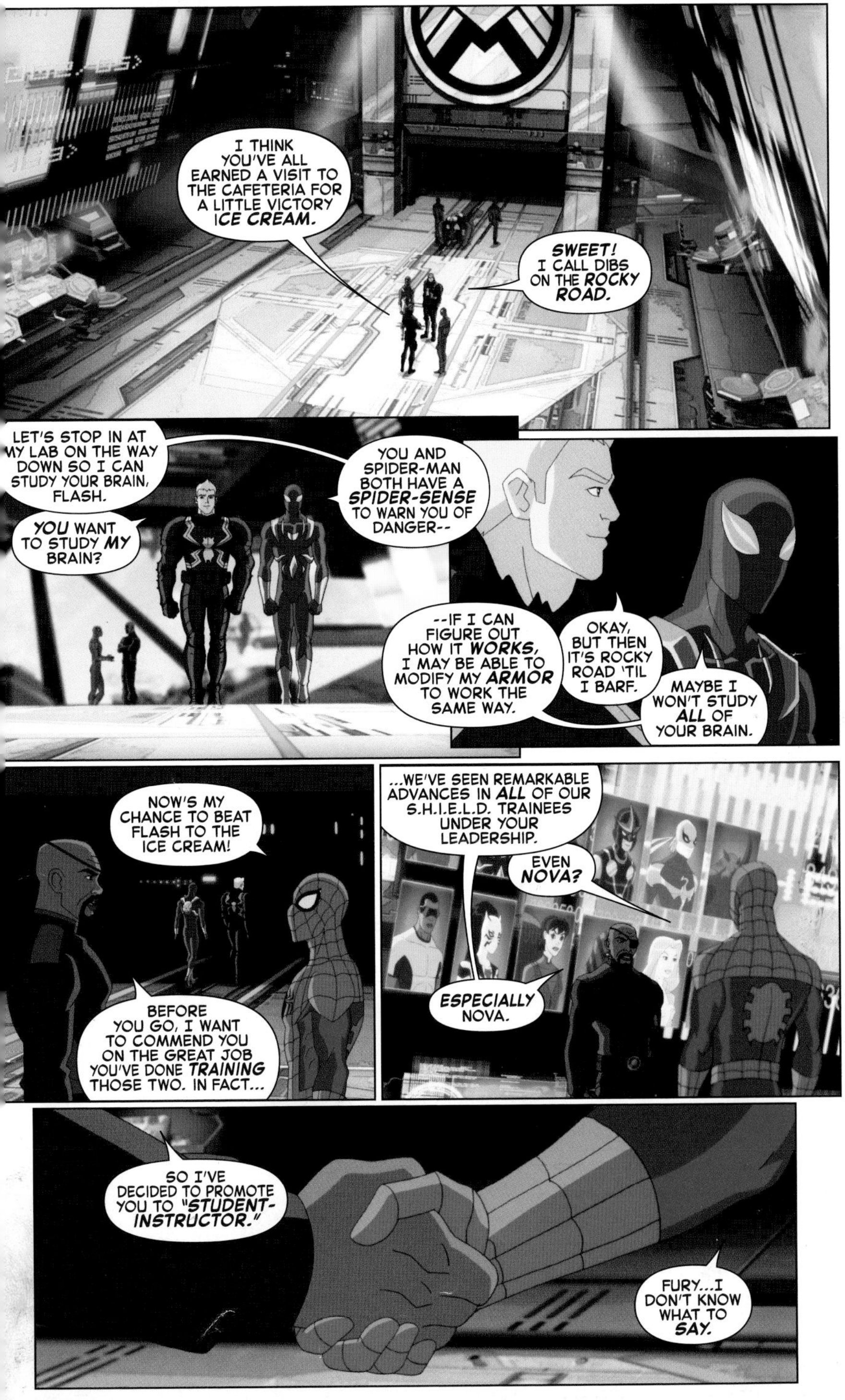
I THINK YOU'VE ALL EARNED A VISIT TO THE CAFETERIA FOR A LITTLE VICTORY ICE CREAM.
SWEET! I CALL DIBS ON THE ROCKY ROAD.
LET'S STOP IN AT MY LAB ON THE WAY DOWN SO I CAN STUDY YOUR BRAIN, FLASH.
YOU WANT TO STUDY MY BRAIN?
YOU AND SPIDER-MAN BOTH HAVE A SPIDER-SENSE TO WARN YOU OF DANGER--
--IF I CAN FIGURE OUT HOW IT WORKS, I MAY BE ABLE TO MODIFY MY ARMOR TO WORK THE SAME WAY.
OKAY, BUT THEN IT'S ROCKY ROAD 'TIL I BARF.
MAYBE I WON'T STUDY ALL OF YOUR BRAIN.
NOW'S MY CHANCE TO BEAT FLASH TO THE ICE CREAM!
BEFORE YOU GO, I WANT TO COMMEND YOU ON THE GREAT JOB YOU'VE DONE TRAINING THOSE TWO. IN FACT...
...WE'VE SEEN REMARKABLE ADVANCES IN ALL OF OUR S.H.I.E.L.D. TRAINEES UNDER YOUR LEADERSHIP.
EVEN NOVA?
ESPECIALLY NOVA.
SO I'VE DECIDED TO PROMOTE YOU TO "STUDENT-INSTRUCTOR."
FURY...I DON'T KNOW WHAT TO SAY.

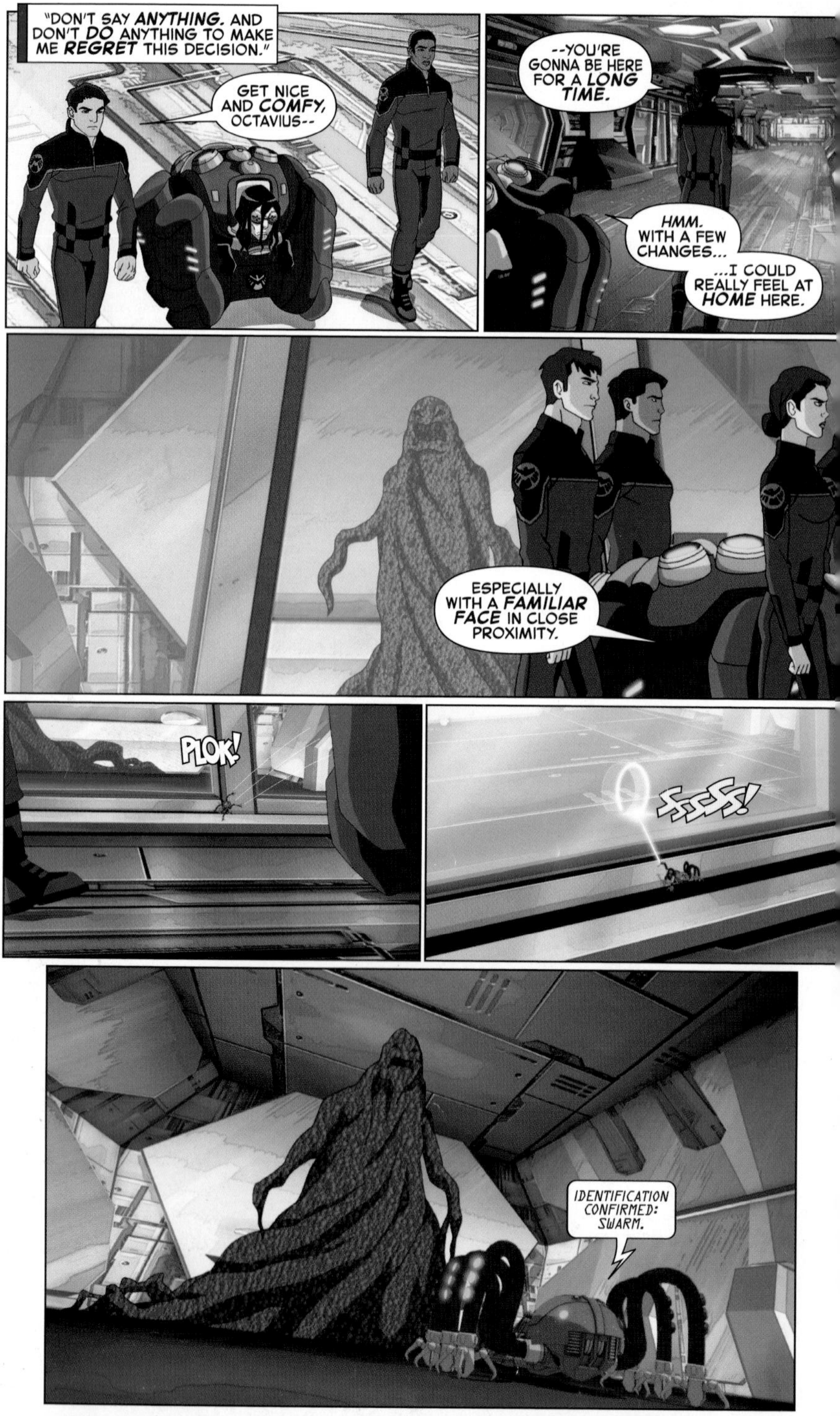
"DON'T SAY ANYTHING. AND DON'T DO ANYTHING TO MAKE ME REGRET THIS DECISION."
GET NICE AND COMFY, OCTAVIUS--
--YOU'RE GONNA BE HERE FOR A LONG TIME.
HMM. WITH A FEW CHANGES...
...I COULD REALLY FEEL AT HOME HERE.
ESPECIALLY WITH A FAMILIAR FACE IN CLOSE PROXIMITY.
PLOK!
SSSS!
IDENTIFICATION CONFIRMED: SWARM.

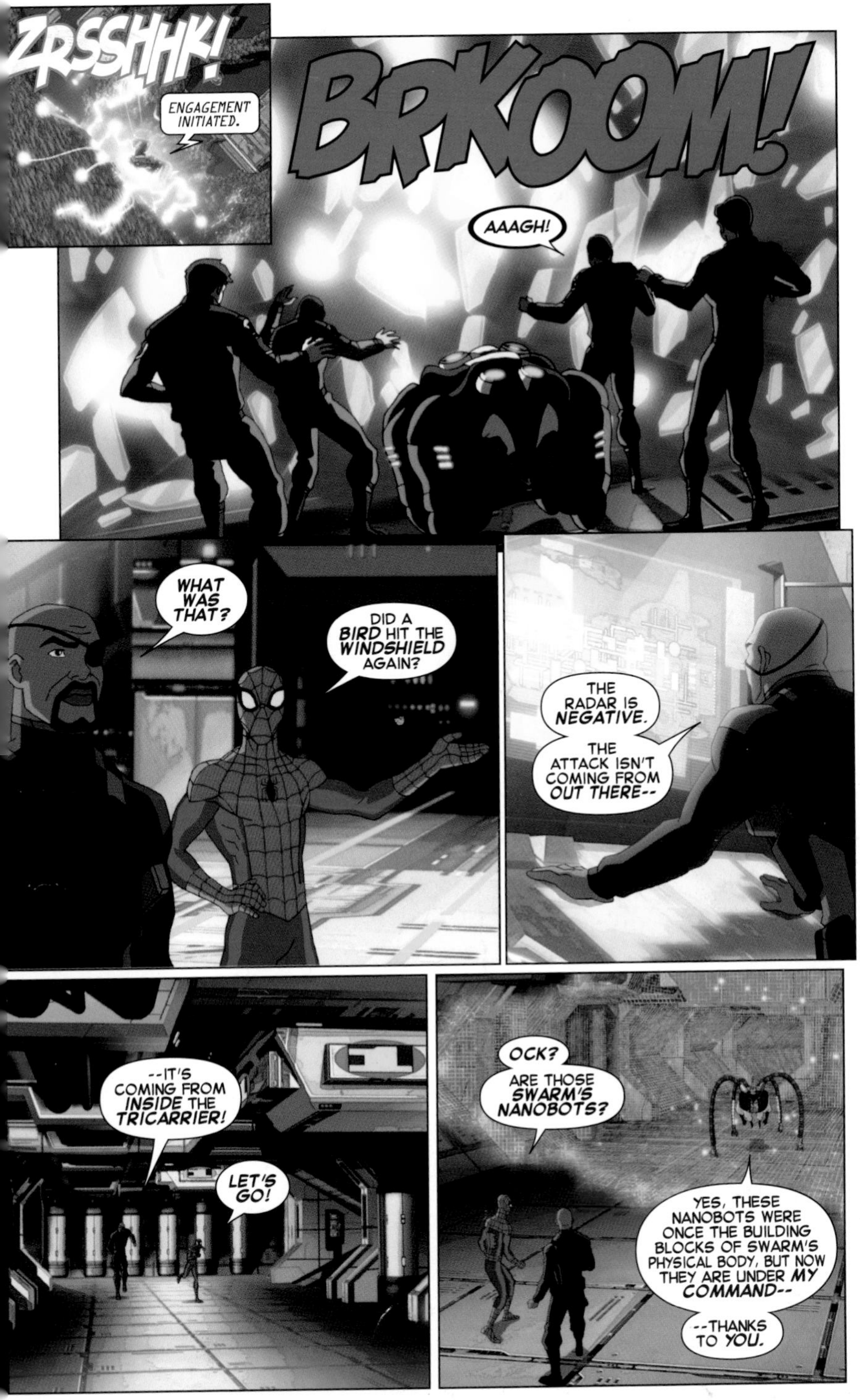
ZRSSHHK!
ENGAGEMENT INITIATED.
BRKOOM!
AAAGH!
WHAT WAS THAT?
DID A BIRD HIT THE WINDSHIELD AGAIN?
THE RADAR IS NEGATIVE.
THE ATTACK ISN'T COMING FROM OUT THERE--
--IT'S COMING FROM INSIDE THE TRICARRIER!
LET'S GO!
OCK?
ARE THOSE SWARM'S NANOBOTS?
YES, THESE NANOBOTS WERE ONCE THE BUILDING BLOCKS OF SWARM'S PHYSICAL BODY, BUT NOW THEY ARE UNDER MY COMMAND--
--THANKS TO YOU.

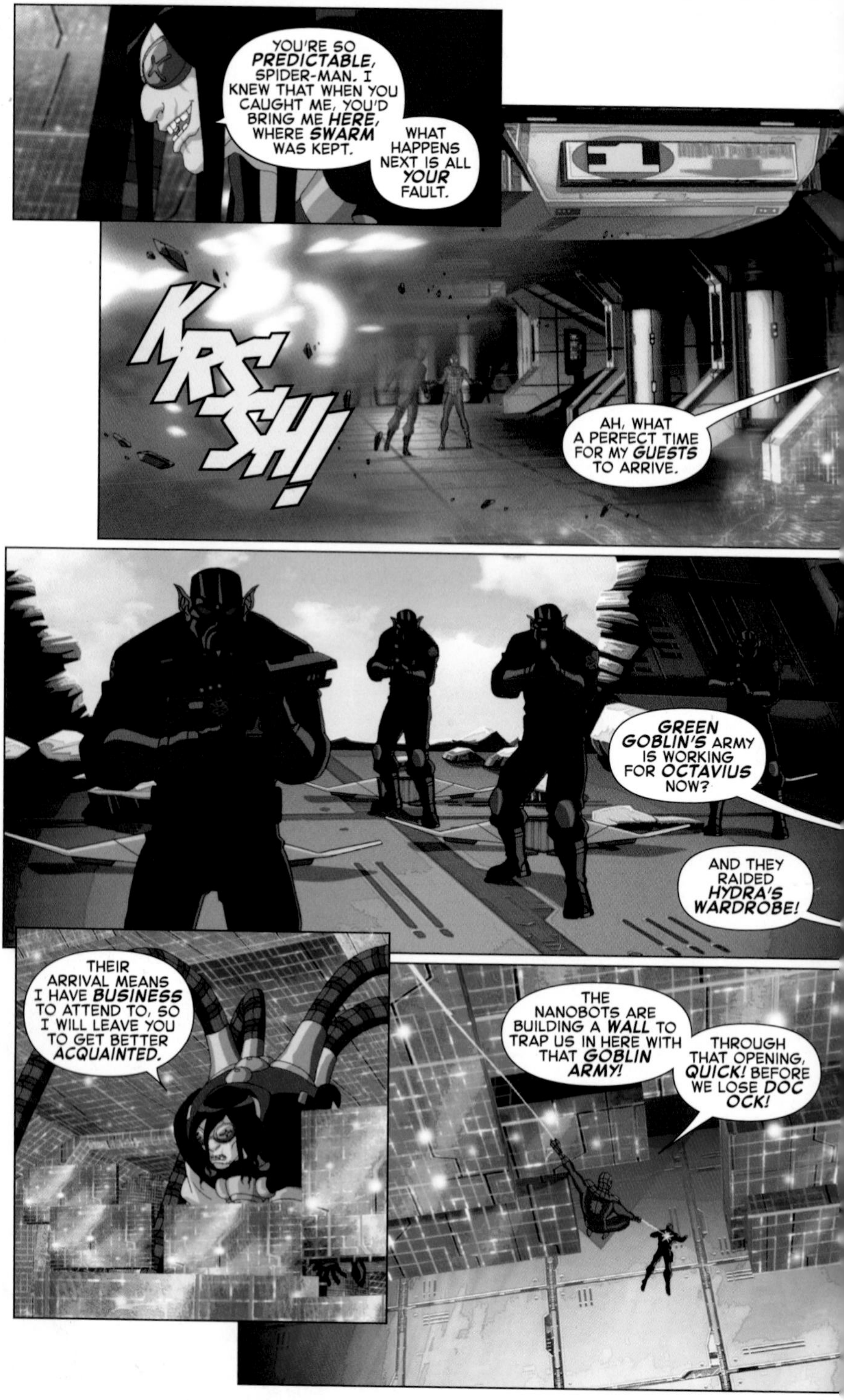
YOU'RE SO PREDICTABLE, SPIDER-MAN. I KNEW THAT WHEN YOU CAUGHT ME, YOU'D BRING ME HERE, WHERE SWARM WAS KEPT.
WHAT HAPPENS NEXT IS ALL YOUR FAULT.
KRSSH!
AH, WHAT A PERFECT TIME FOR MY GUESTS TO ARRIVE.
GREEN GOBLIN'S ARMY IS WORKING FOR OCTAVIUS NOW?
AND THEY RAIDED HYDRA'S WARDROBE!
THEIR ARRIVAL MEANS I HAVE BUSINESS TO ATTEND TO, SO I WILL LEAVE YOU TO GET BETTER ACQUAINTED.
THE NANOBOTS ARE BUILDING A WALL TO TRAP US IN HERE WITH THAT GOBLIN ARMY!
THROUGH THAT OPENING, QUICK! BEFORE WE LOSE DOC OCK!

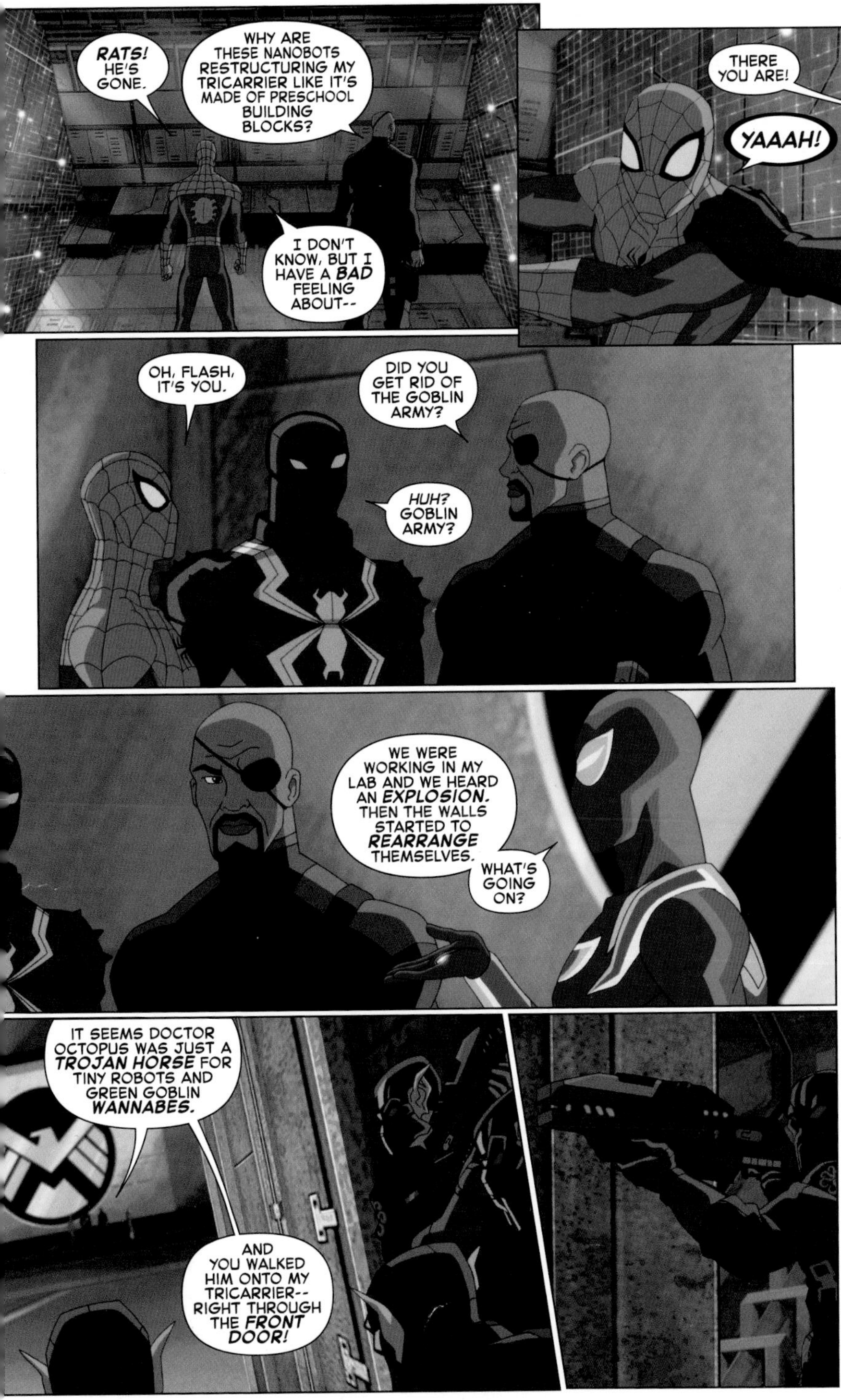
RATS! HE'S GONE.
WHY ARE THESE NANOBOTS RESTRUCTURING MY TRICARRIER LIKE IT'S MADE OF PRESCHOOL BUILDING BLOCKS?
I DON'T KNOW, BUT I HAVE A BAD FEELING ABOUT--
THERE YOU ARE!
YAAAH!
OH, FLASH, IT'S YOU.
DID YOU GET RID OF THE GOBLIN ARMY?
HUH? GOBLIN ARMY?
WE WERE WORKING IN MY LAB AND WE HEARD AN EXPLOSION. THEN THE WALLS STARTED TO REARRANGE THEMSELVES.
WHAT'S GOING ON?
IT SEEMS DOCTOR OCTOPUS WAS JUST A TROJAN HORSE FOR TINY ROBOTS AND GREEN GOBLIN WANNABES.
AND YOU WALKED HIM ONTO MY TRICARRIER-- RIGHT THROUGH THE FRONT DOOR!

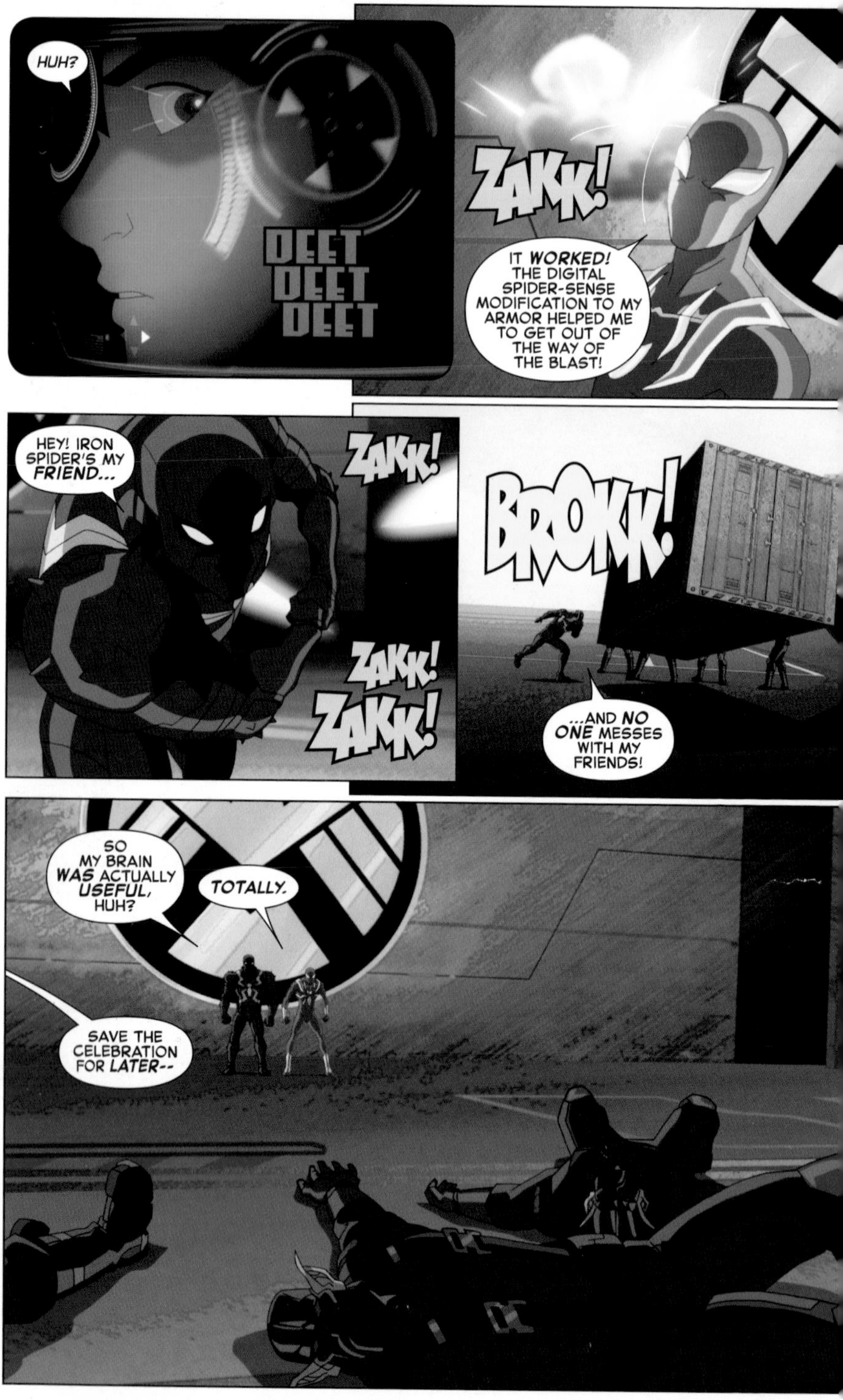
HUH?
DEET DEET DEET
ZAKK!
IT WORKED! THE DIGITAL SPIDER-SENSE MODIFICATION TO MY ARMOR HELPED ME TO GET OUT OF THE WAY OF THE BLAST!
HEY! IRON SPIDER'S MY FRIEND...
ZAKK!
ZAKK!
ZAKK!
BROKK!
...AND NO ONE MESSES WITH MY FRIENDS!
SO MY BRAIN WAS ACTUALLY USEFUL, HUH?
TOTALLY.
SAVE THE CELEBRATION FOR LATER--

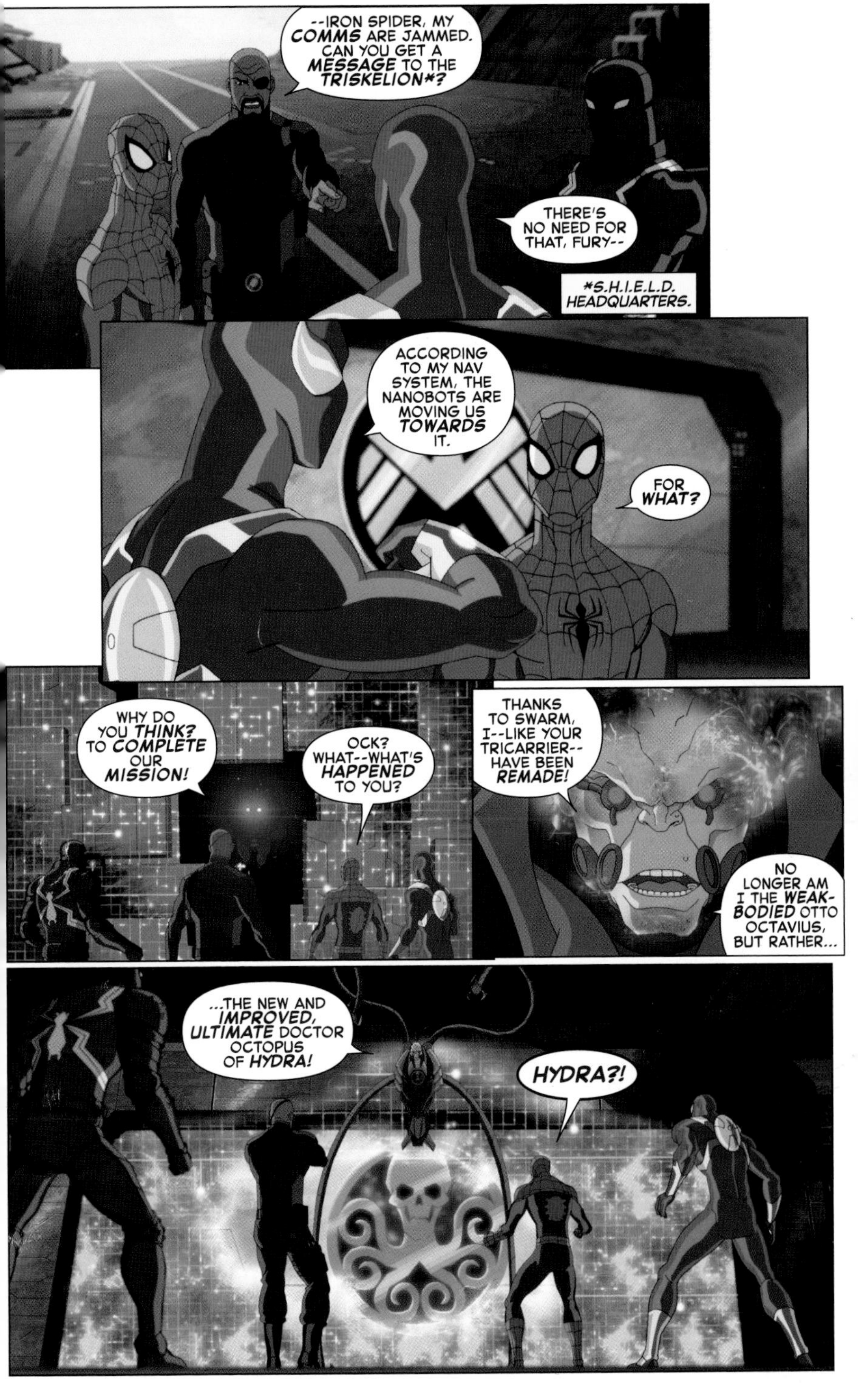
--IRON SPIDER, MY COMMS ARE JAMMED. CAN YOU GET A MESSAGE TO THE TRISKELION*?
THERE'S NO NEED FOR THAT, FURY--
*S.H.I.E.L.D. HEADQUARTERS.
ACCORDING TO MY NAV SYSTEM, THE NANOBOTS ARE MOVING US TOWARDS IT.
FOR WHAT?
WHY DO YOU THINK? TO COMPLETE OUR MISSION!
OCK? WHAT--WHAT'S HAPPENED TO YOU?
THANKS TO SWARM, I--LIKE YOUR TRICARRIER--HAVE BEEN REMADE!
NO LONGER AM I THE WEAK-BODIED OTTO OCTAVIUS, BUT RATHER...
...THE NEW AND IMPROVED, ULTIMATE DOCTOR OCTOPUS OF HYDRA!
HYDRA?!

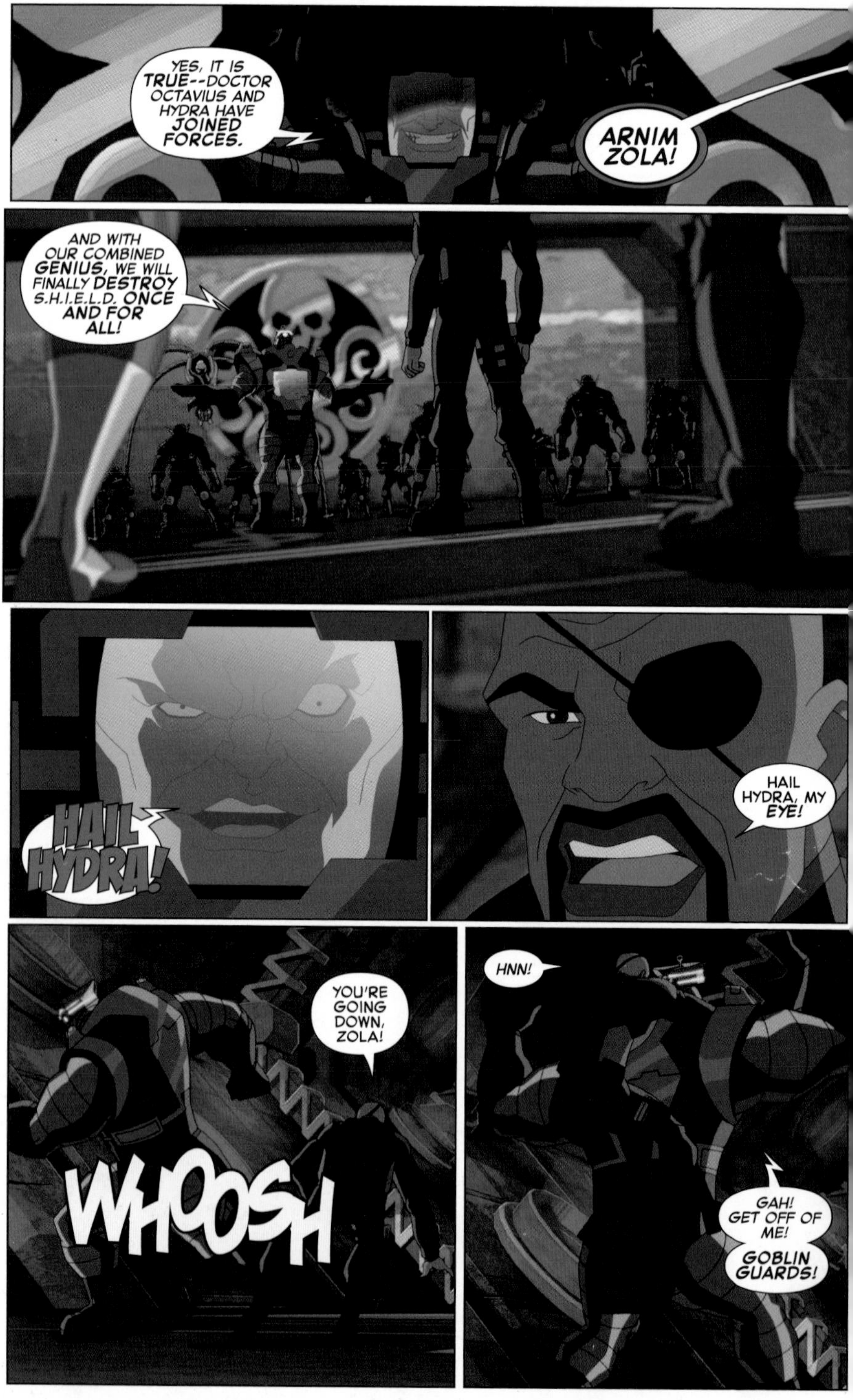
YES, IT IS TRUE--DOCTOR OCTAVIUS AND HYDRA HAVE JOINED FORCES.
ARNIM ZOLA!
AND WITH OUR COMBINED GENIUS, WE WILL FINALLY DESTROY S.H.I.E.L.D. ONCE AND FOR ALL!
HAIL HYDRA!
HAIL HYDRA, MY EYE!
YOU'RE GOING DOWN, ZOLA!
WHOOSH
HNN!
GAH! GET OFF OF ME!
GOBLIN GUARDS!

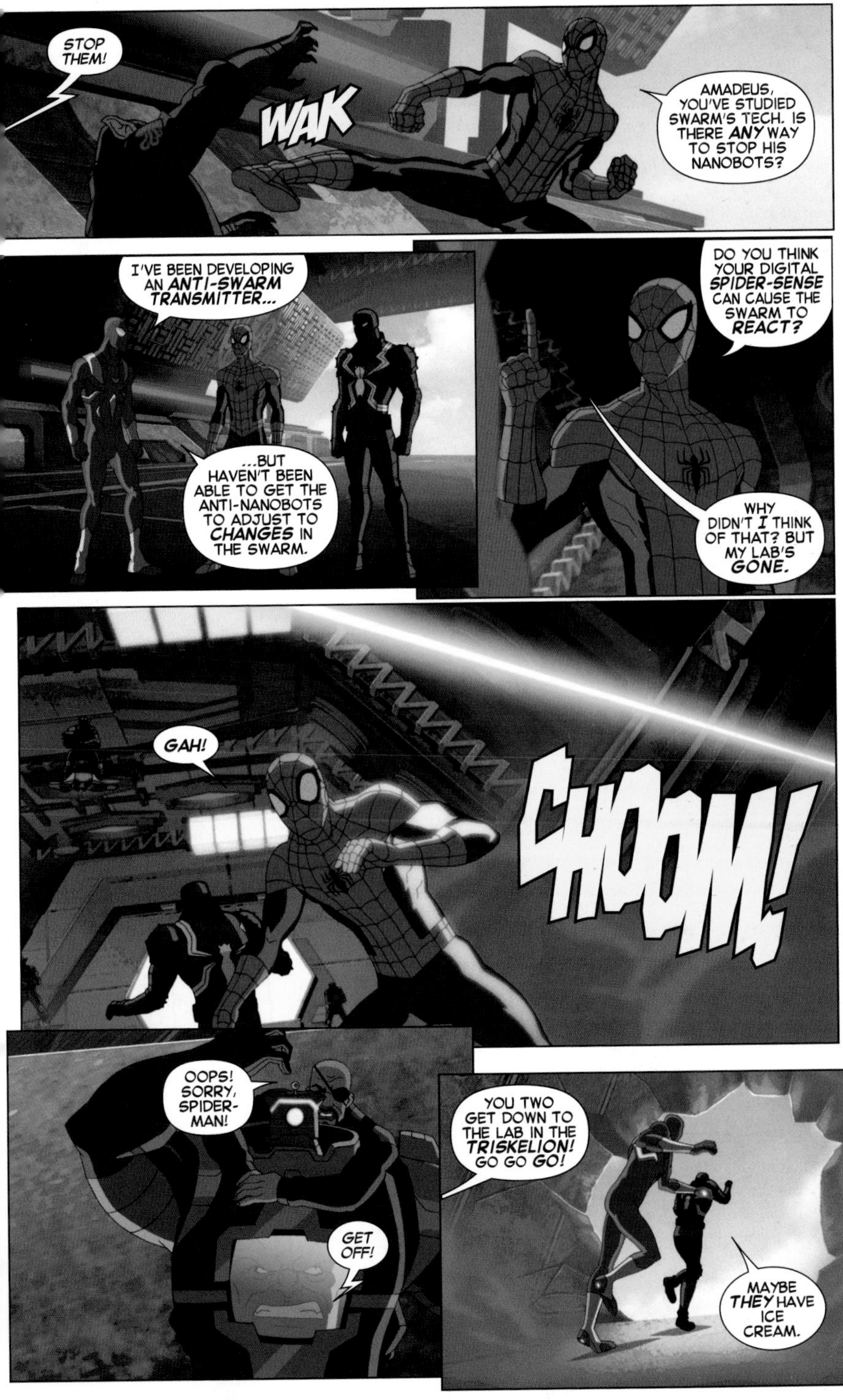
STOP THEM!
WAK
AMADEUS, YOU'VE STUDIED SWARM'S TECH. IS THERE ANY WAY TO STOP HIS NANOBOTS?
I'VE BEEN DEVELOPING AN ANTI-SWARM TRANSMITTER...
...BUT HAVEN'T BEEN ABLE TO GET THE ANTI-NANOBOTS TO ADJUST TO CHANGES IN THE SWARM.
DO YOU THINK YOUR DIGITAL SPIDER-SENSE CAN CAUSE THE SWARM TO REACT?
WHY DIDN'T I THINK OF THAT? BUT MY LAB'S GONE.
GAH!
CHOOM!
OOPS! SORRY, SPIDER-MAN!
GET OFF!
YOU TWO GET DOWN TO THE LAB IN THE TRISKELION! GO GO GO!
MAYBE THEY HAVE ICE CREAM.

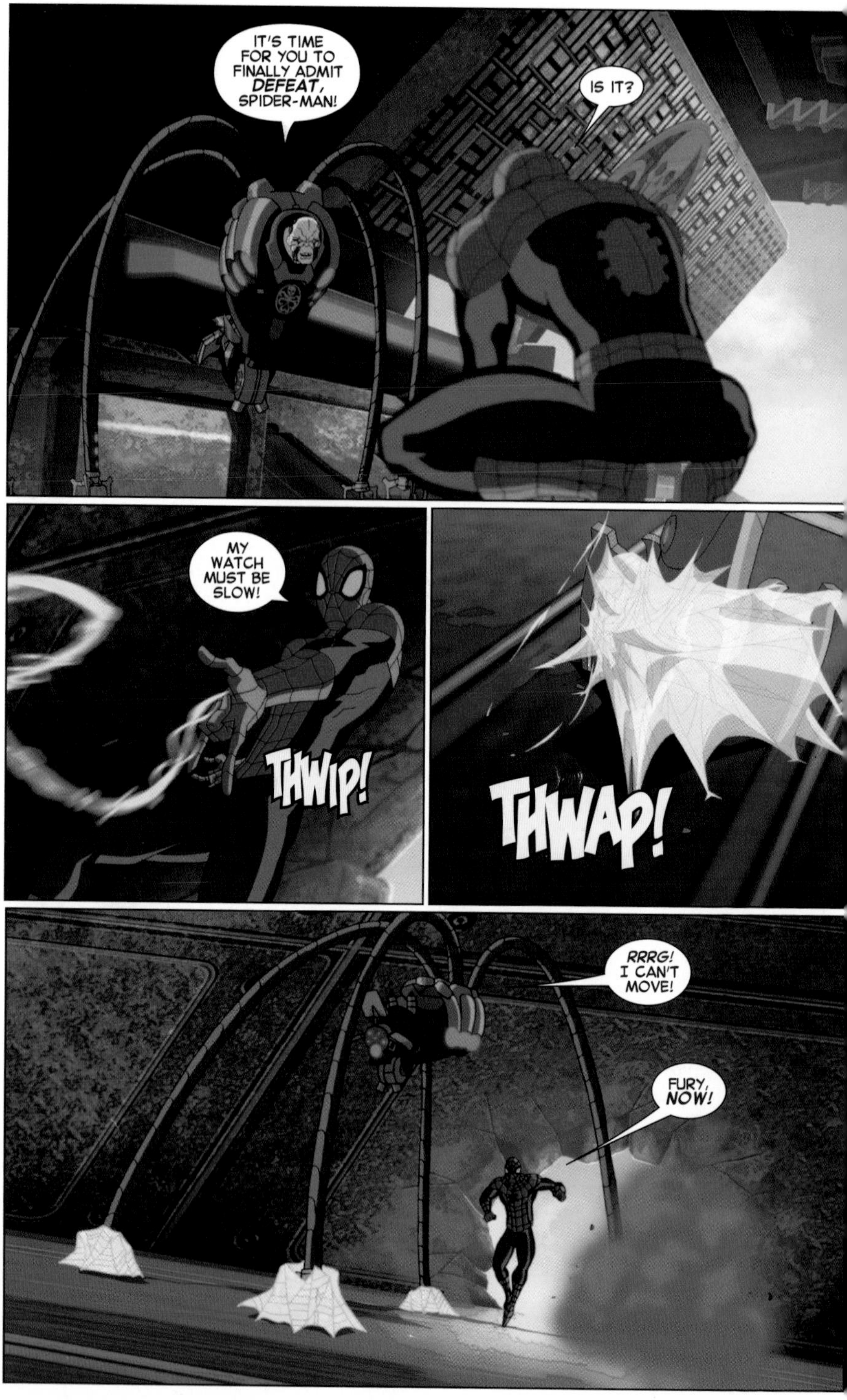
IT'S TIME FOR YOU TO FINALLY ADMIT *DEFEAT*, SPIDER-MAN!
IS IT?
MY WATCH MUST BE SLOW!
THWIP!
THWAP!
RRRG! I CAN'T MOVE!
FURY, *NOW!*

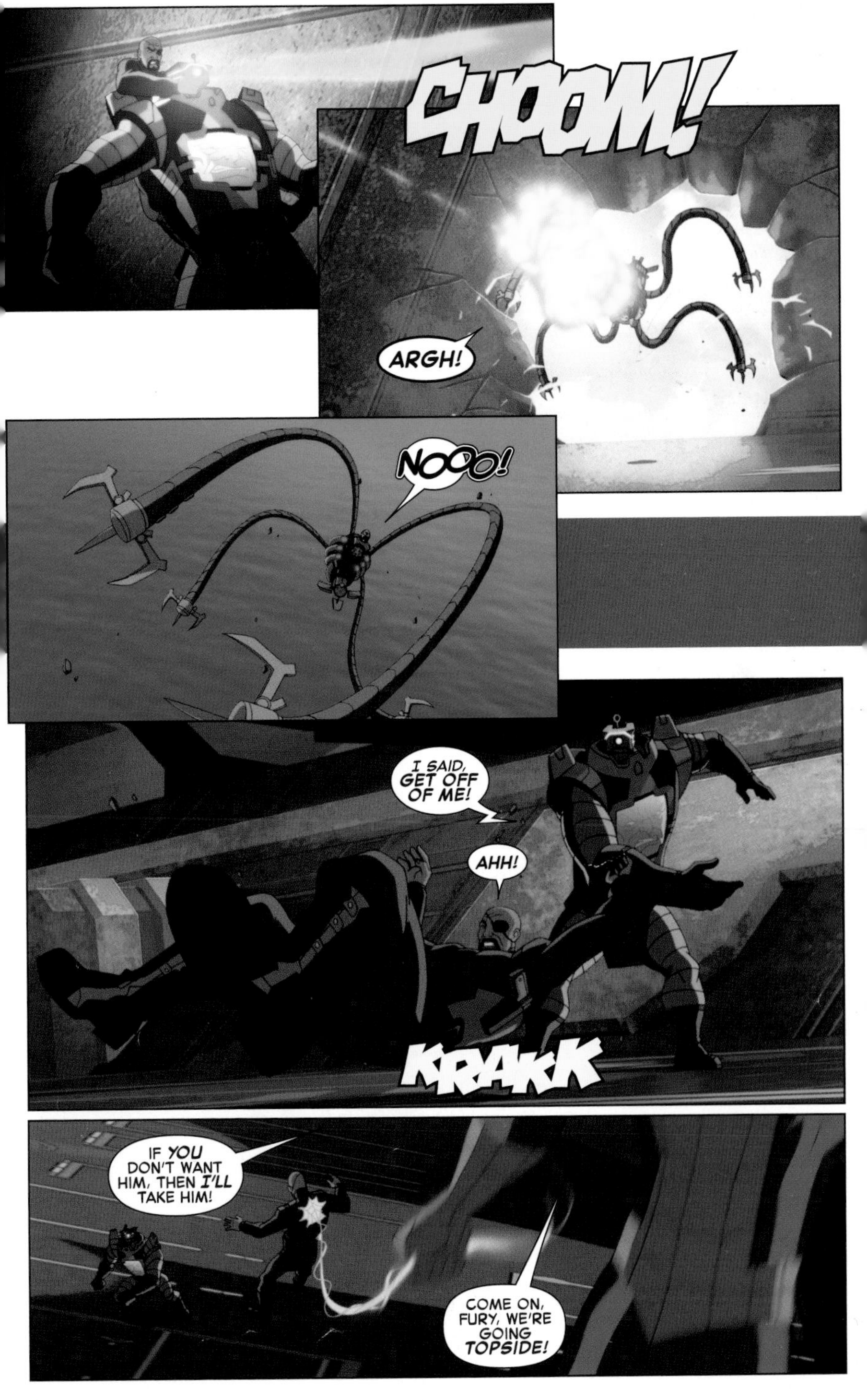
CHOOM!
ARGH!
NOOO!
I SAID, GET OFF OF ME!
AHH!
KRAKK
IF YOU DON'T WANT HIM, THEN I'LL TAKE HIM!
COME ON, FURY, WE'RE GOING TOPSIDE!

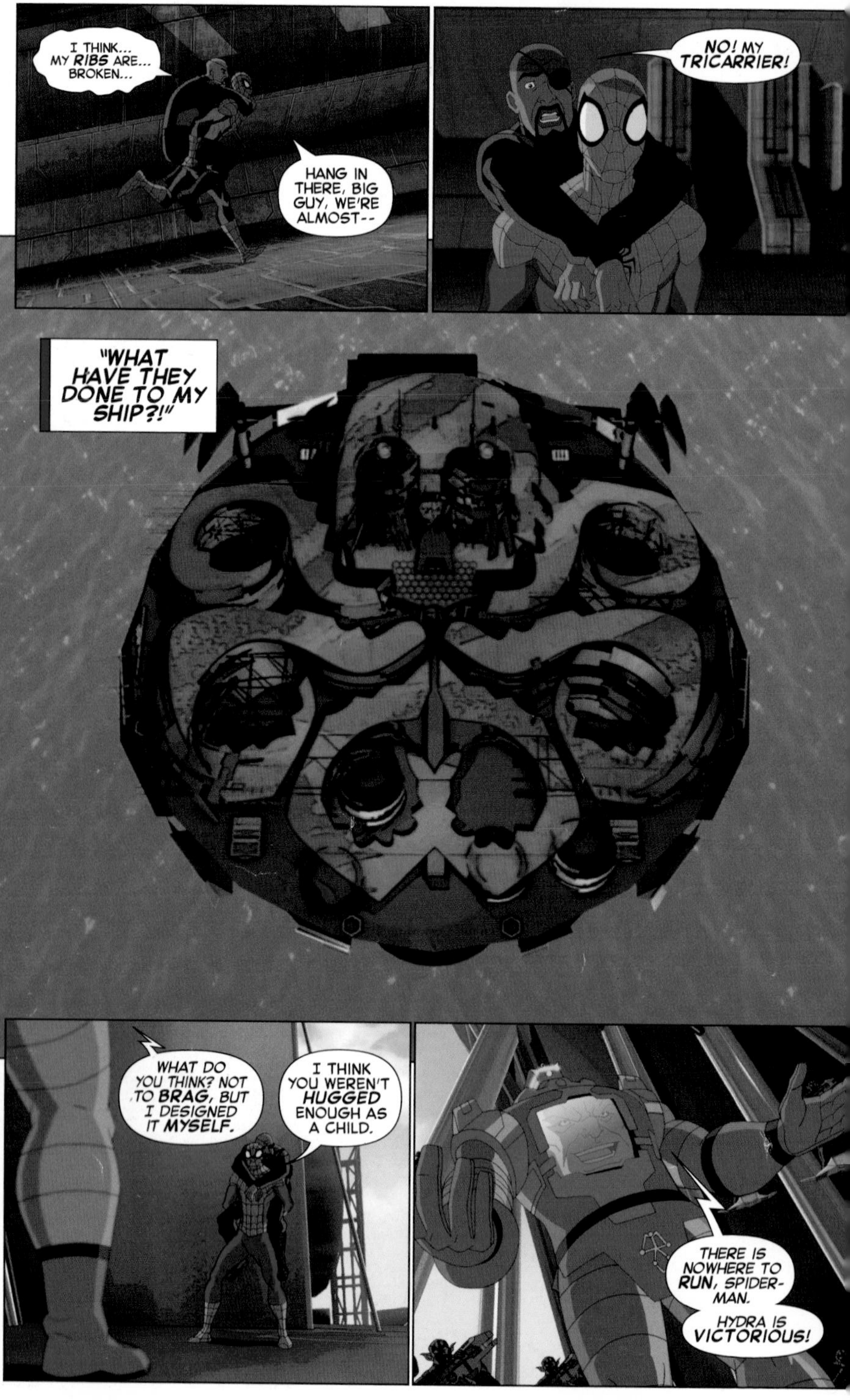
I THINK... MY RIBS ARE... BROKEN...
HANG IN THERE, BIG GUY, WE'RE ALMOST--
NO! MY TRICARRIER!
"WHAT HAVE THEY DONE TO MY SHIP?!"
WHAT DO YOU THINK? NOT TO BRAG, BUT I DESIGNED IT MYSELF.
I THINK YOU WEREN'T HUGGED ENOUGH AS A CHILD.
THERE IS NOWHERE TO RUN, SPIDER-MAN.
HYDRA IS VICTORIOUS!

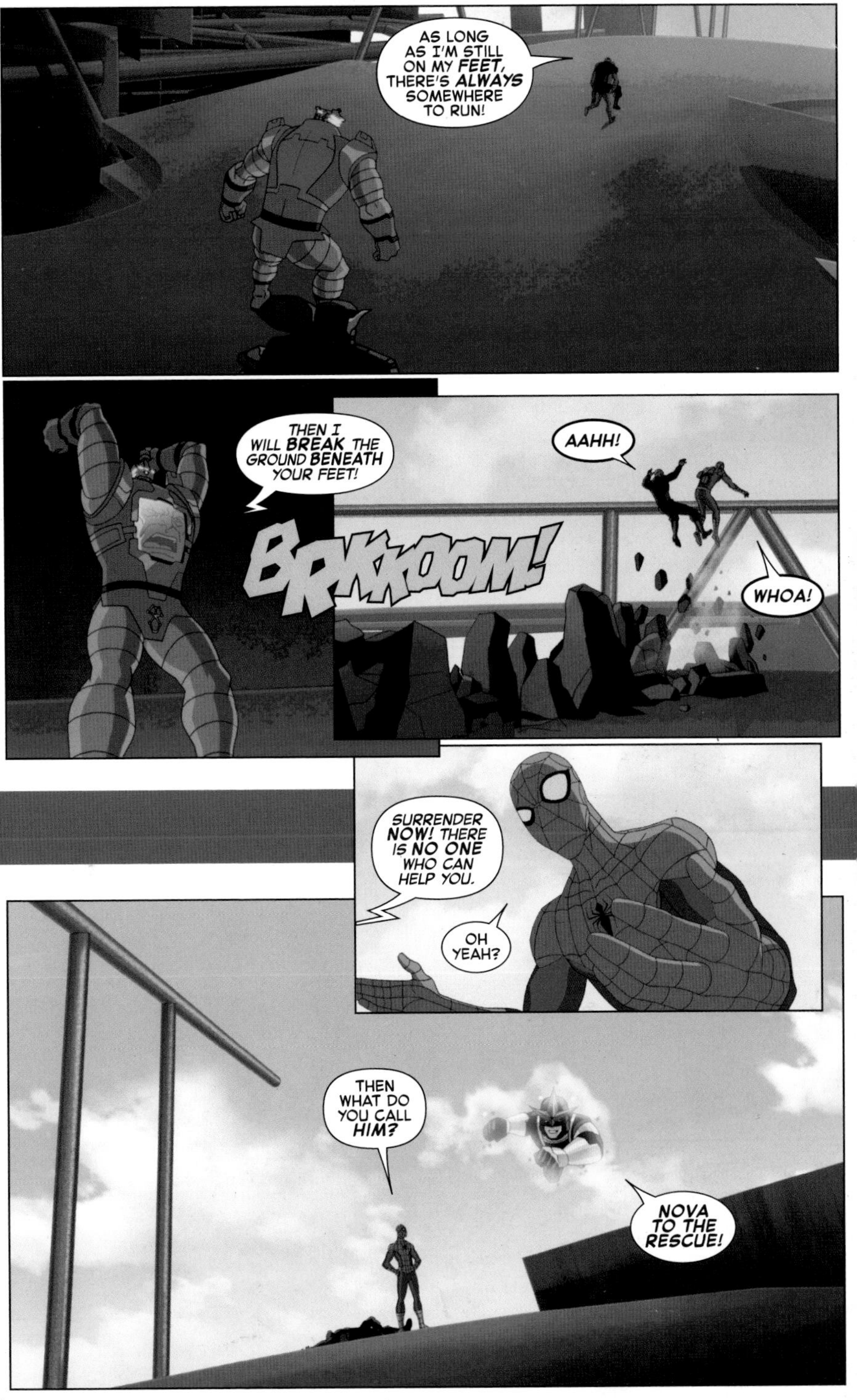
AS LONG AS I'M STILL ON MY FEET, THERE'S ALWAYS SOMEWHERE TO RUN!
THEN I WILL BREAK THE GROUND BENEATH YOUR FEET!
BRKKOOM!
AAHH!
WHOA!
SURRENDER NOW! THERE IS NO ONE WHO CAN HELP YOU.
OH YEAH?
THEN WHAT DO YOU CALL HIM?
NOVA TO THE RESCUE!

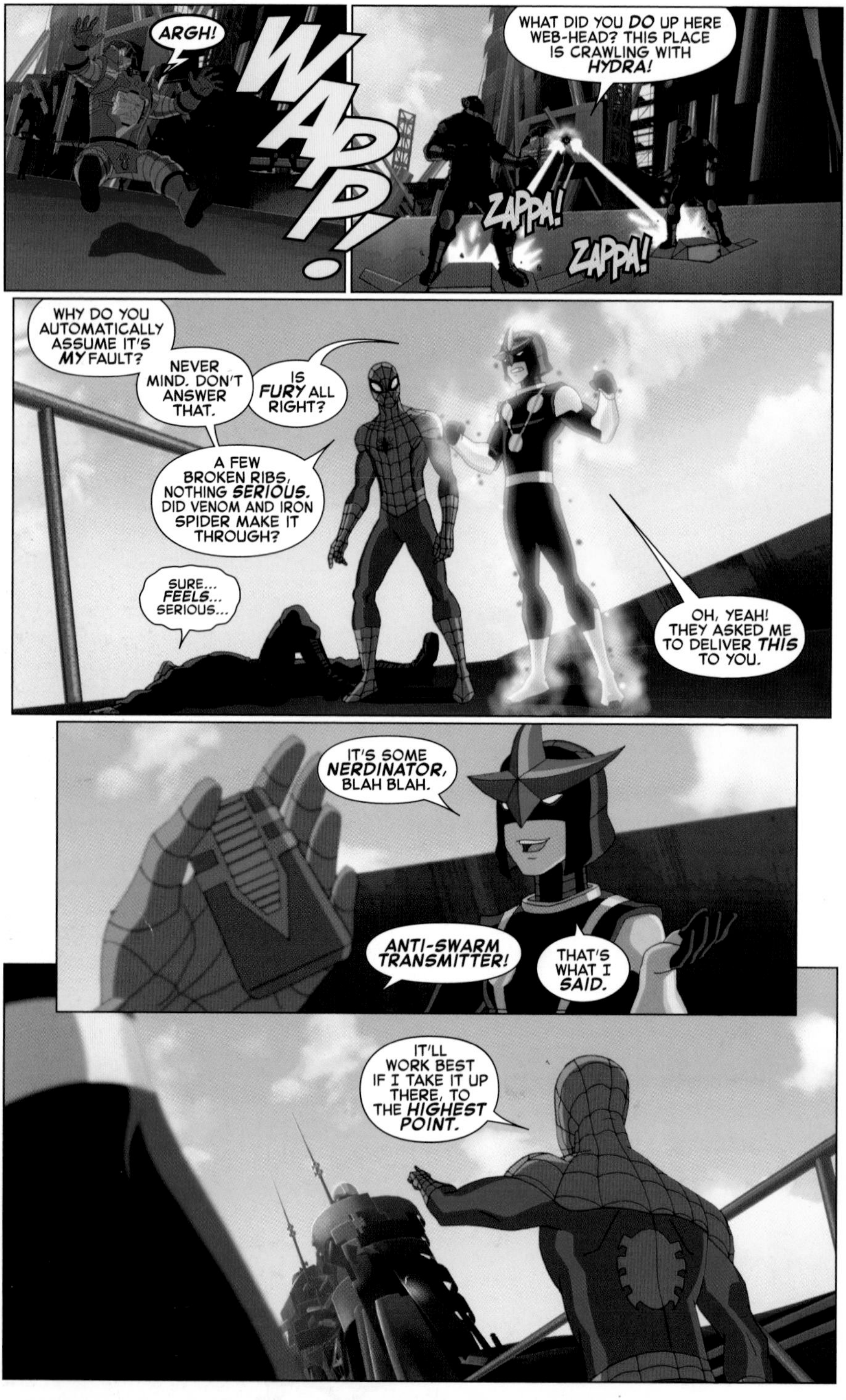
ARGH!
WAP!
WHAT DID YOU DO UP HERE WEB-HEAD? THIS PLACE IS CRAWLING WITH HYDRA!
ZAPPA!
ZAPPA!
WHY DO YOU AUTOMATICALLY ASSUME IT'S MY FAULT?
NEVER MIND. DON'T ANSWER THAT.
IS FURY ALL RIGHT?
A FEW BROKEN RIBS, NOTHING SERIOUS. DID VENOM AND IRON SPIDER MAKE IT THROUGH?
SURE... FEELS... SERIOUS...
OH, YEAH! THEY ASKED ME TO DELIVER THIS TO YOU.
IT'S SOME NERDINATOR, BLAH BLAH.
ANTI-SWARM TRANSMITTER!
THAT'S WHAT I SAID.
IT'LL WORK BEST IF I TAKE IT UP THERE, TO THE HIGHEST POINT.

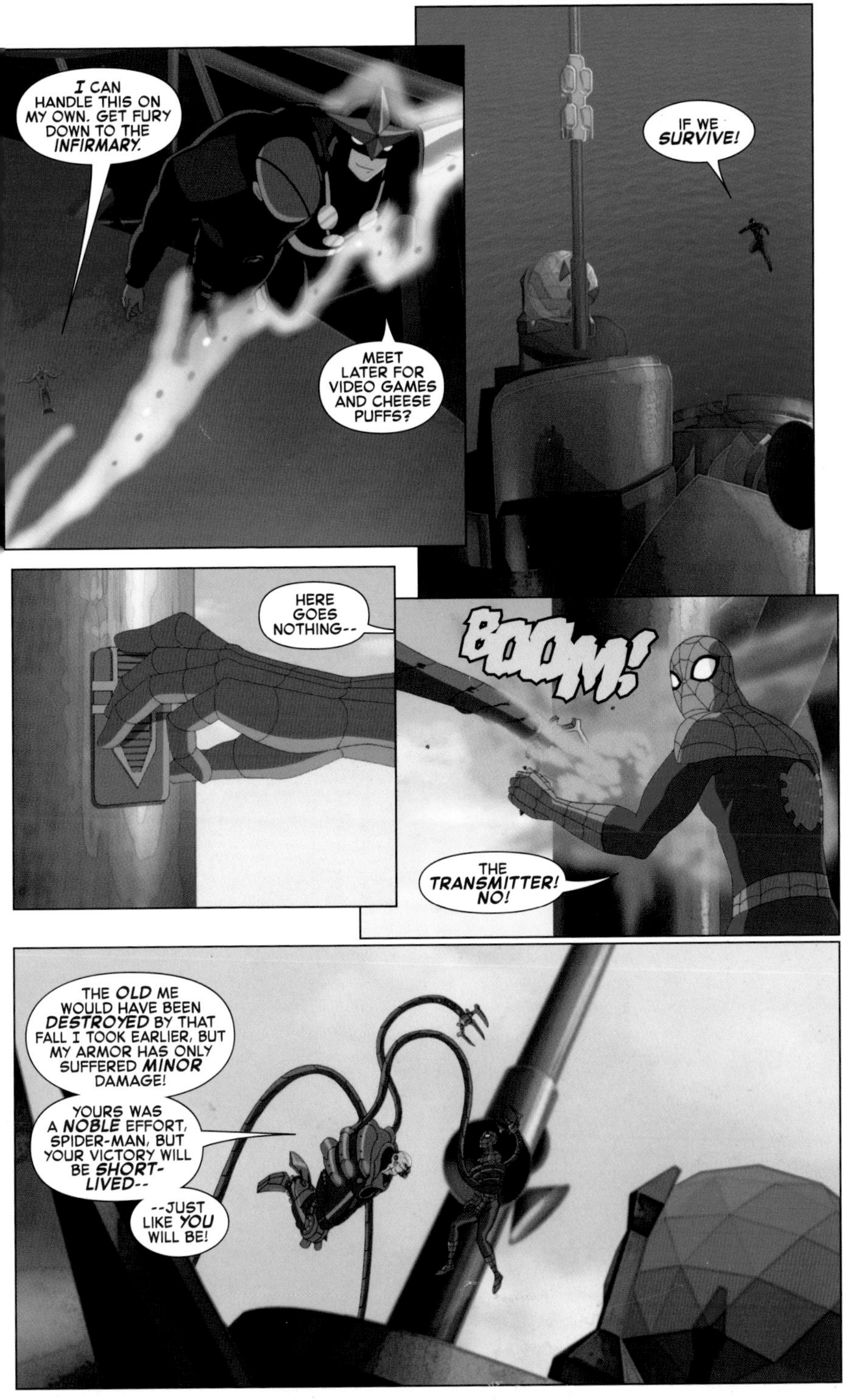
I CAN HANDLE THIS ON MY OWN. GET FURY DOWN TO THE INFIRMARY.
MEET LATER FOR VIDEO GAMES AND CHEESE PUFFS?
IF WE SURVIVE!
HERE GOES NOTHING--
BOOM!
THE TRANSMITTER! NO!
THE OLD ME WOULD HAVE BEEN DESTROYED BY THAT FALL I TOOK EARLIER, BUT MY ARMOR HAS ONLY SUFFERED MINOR DAMAGE!
YOURS WAS A NOBLE EFFORT, SPIDER-MAN, BUT YOUR VICTORY WILL BE SHORT-LIVED--
--JUST LIKE YOU WILL BE!

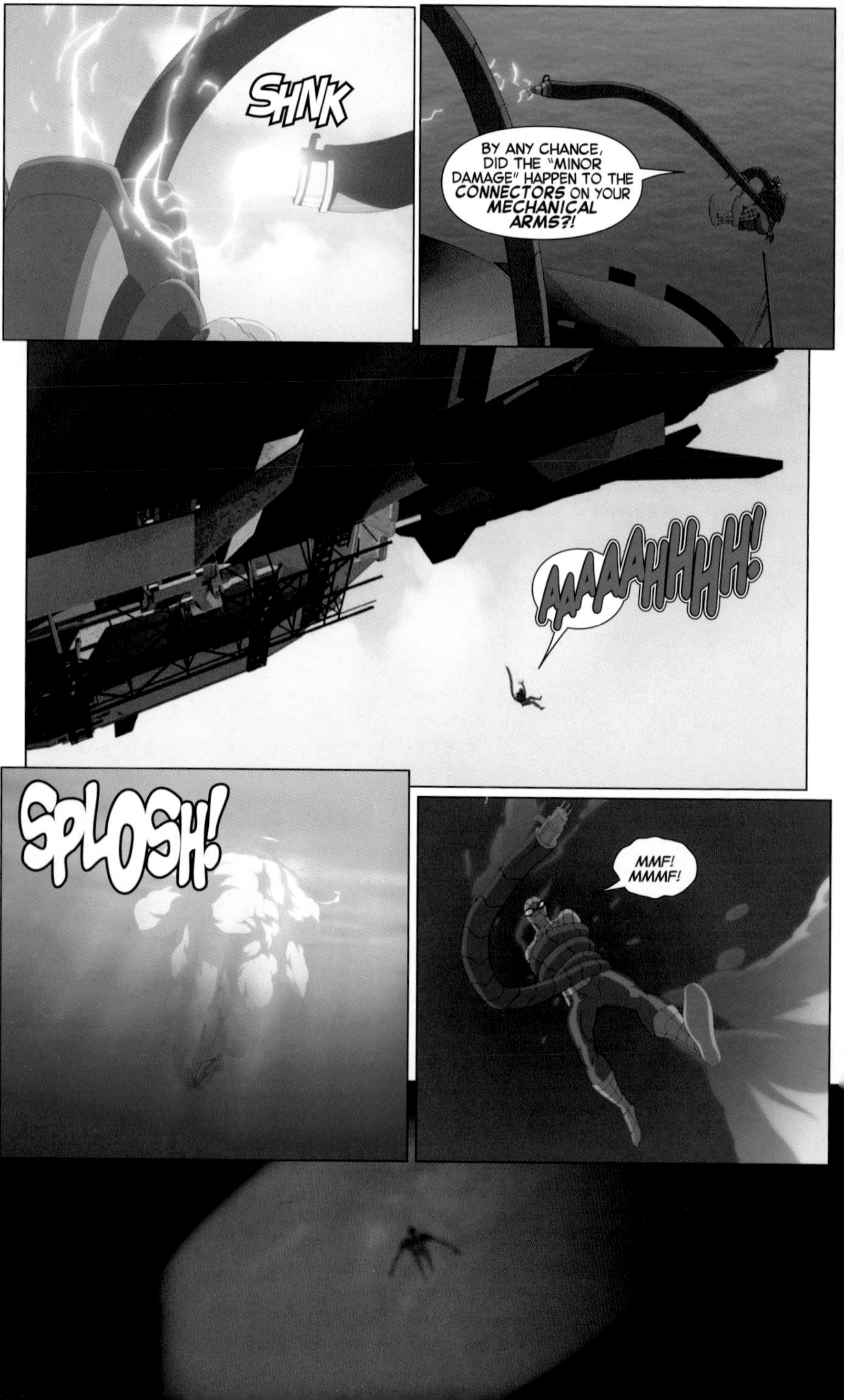
SHNK
BY ANY CHANCE, DID THE "MINOR DAMAGE" HAPPEN TO THE CONNECTORS ON YOUR MECHANICAL ARMS?!
AAAAAHHHH!
SPLOSH!
MMF! MMMF!

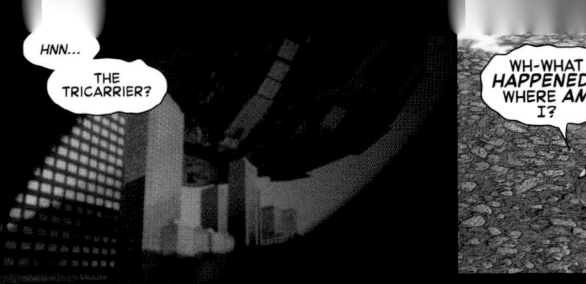

HNN...

THE TRICARRIER?

WH-WHAT *HAPPENED?* WHERE *AM* I?

NO! IT'S ALL GONE-- MY FRIENDS, S.H.I.E.L.D., *EVERYTHING!*

BUT *YOU'RE* NOT.

HUH? WHO ARE YOU?

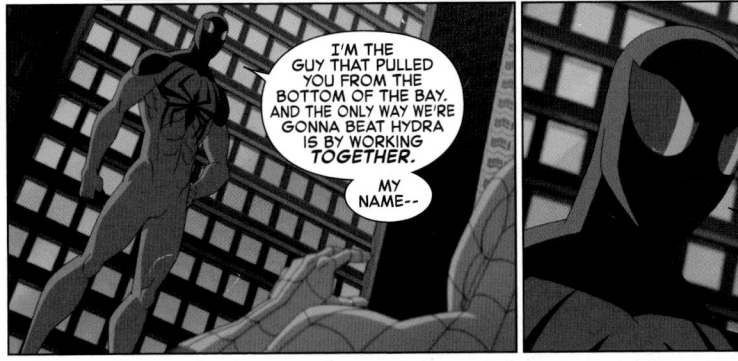

I'M THE GUY THAT PULLED YOU FROM THE BOTTOM OF THE BAY. AND THE ONLY WAY WE'RE GONNA BEAT HYDRA IS BY WORKING *TOGETHER.*

MY NAME--

--IS THE *SCARLET SPIDER.*

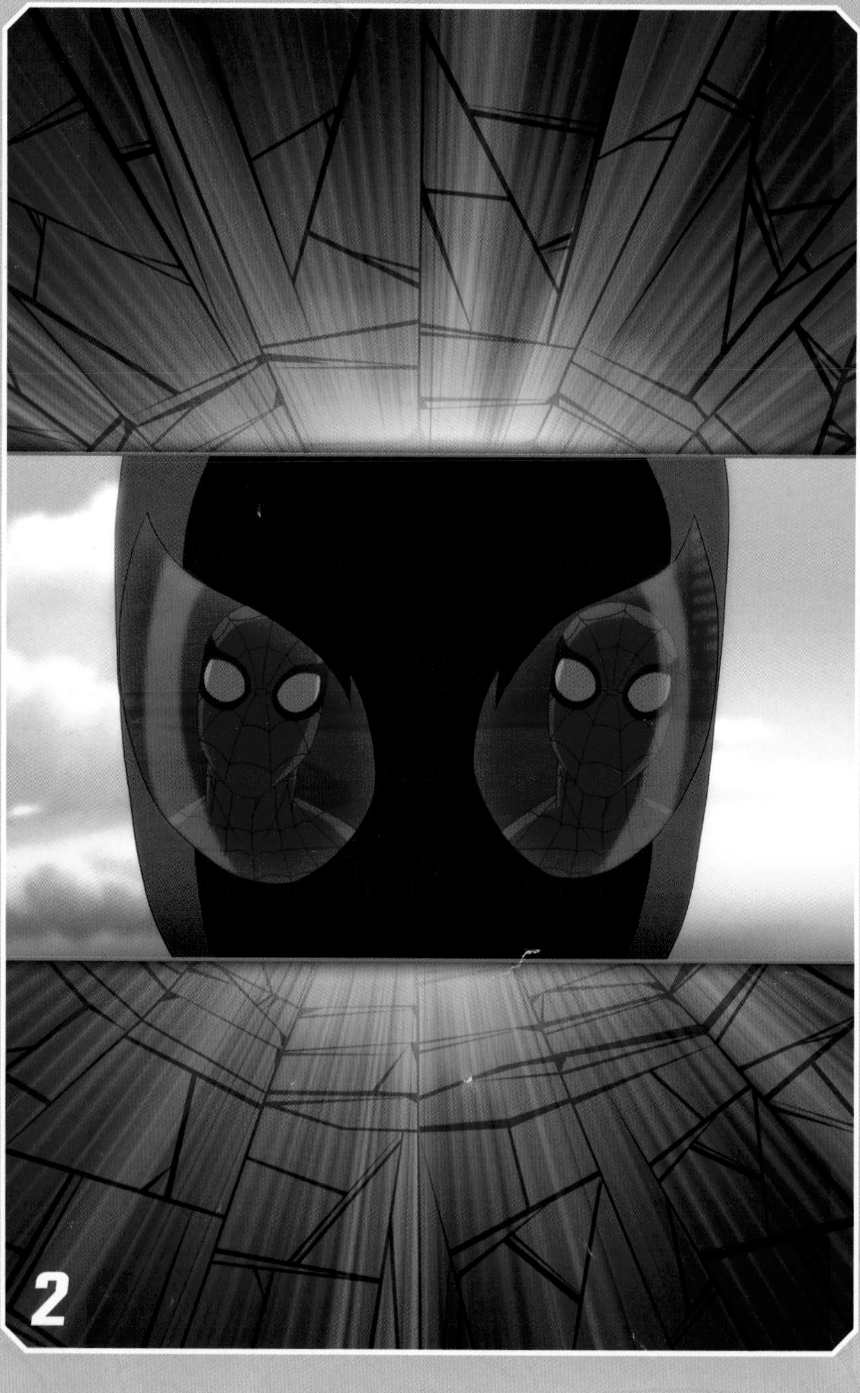

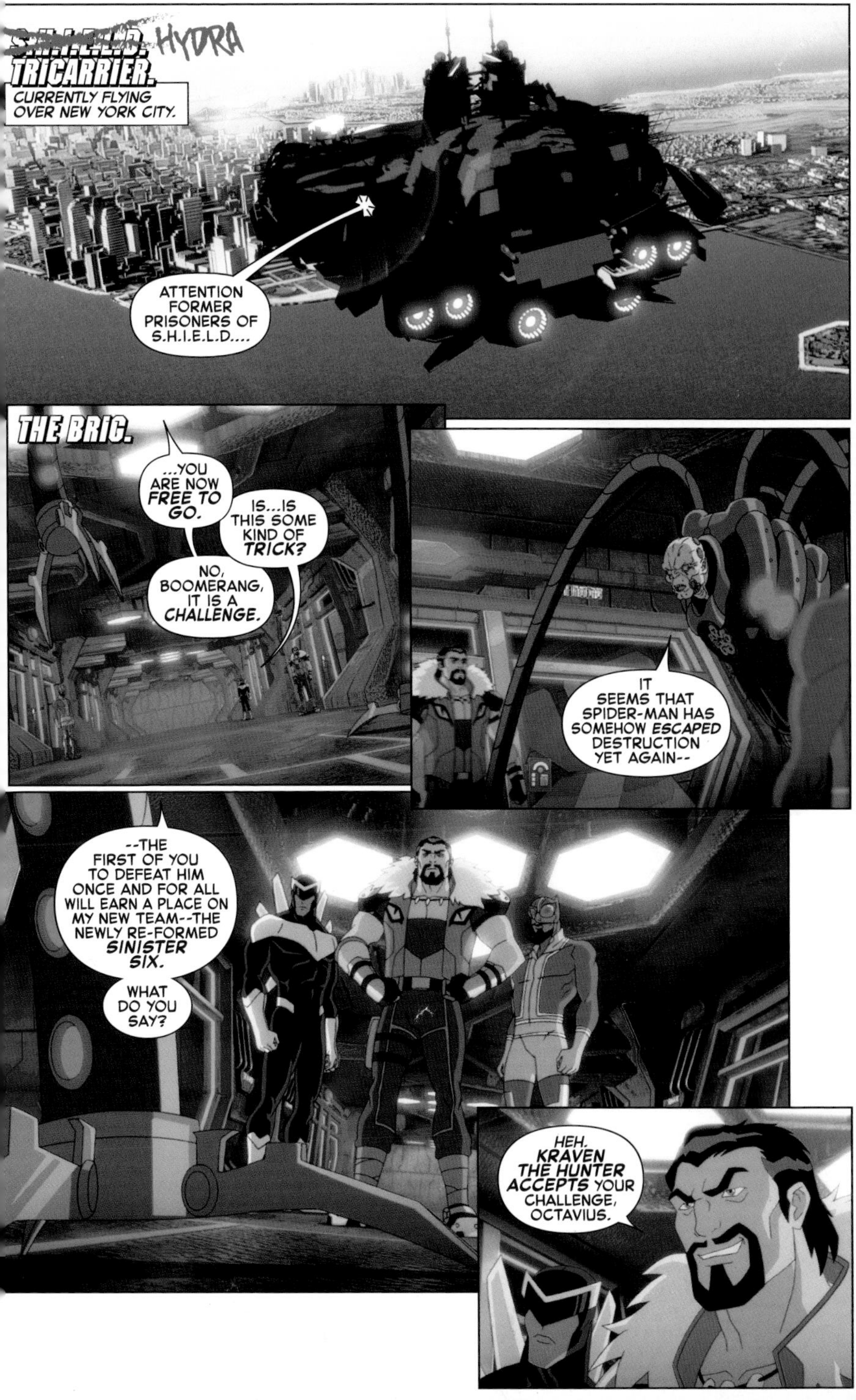

S.H.I.E.L.D. HYDRA TRICARRIER.
CURRENTLY FLYING OVER NEW YORK CITY.
ATTENTION FORMER PRISONERS OF S.H.I.E.L.D....
THE BRIG.
...YOU ARE NOW FREE TO GO.
IS...IS THIS SOME KIND OF TRICK?
NO, BOOMERANG, IT IS A CHALLENGE.
IT SEEMS THAT SPIDER-MAN HAS SOMEHOW ESCAPED DESTRUCTION YET AGAIN--
--THE FIRST OF YOU TO DEFEAT HIM ONCE AND FOR ALL WILL EARN A PLACE ON MY NEW TEAM--THE NEWLY RE-FORMED SINISTER SIX.
WHAT DO YOU SAY?
HEH. KRAVEN THE HUNTER ACCEPTS YOUR CHALLENGE, OCTAVIUS.

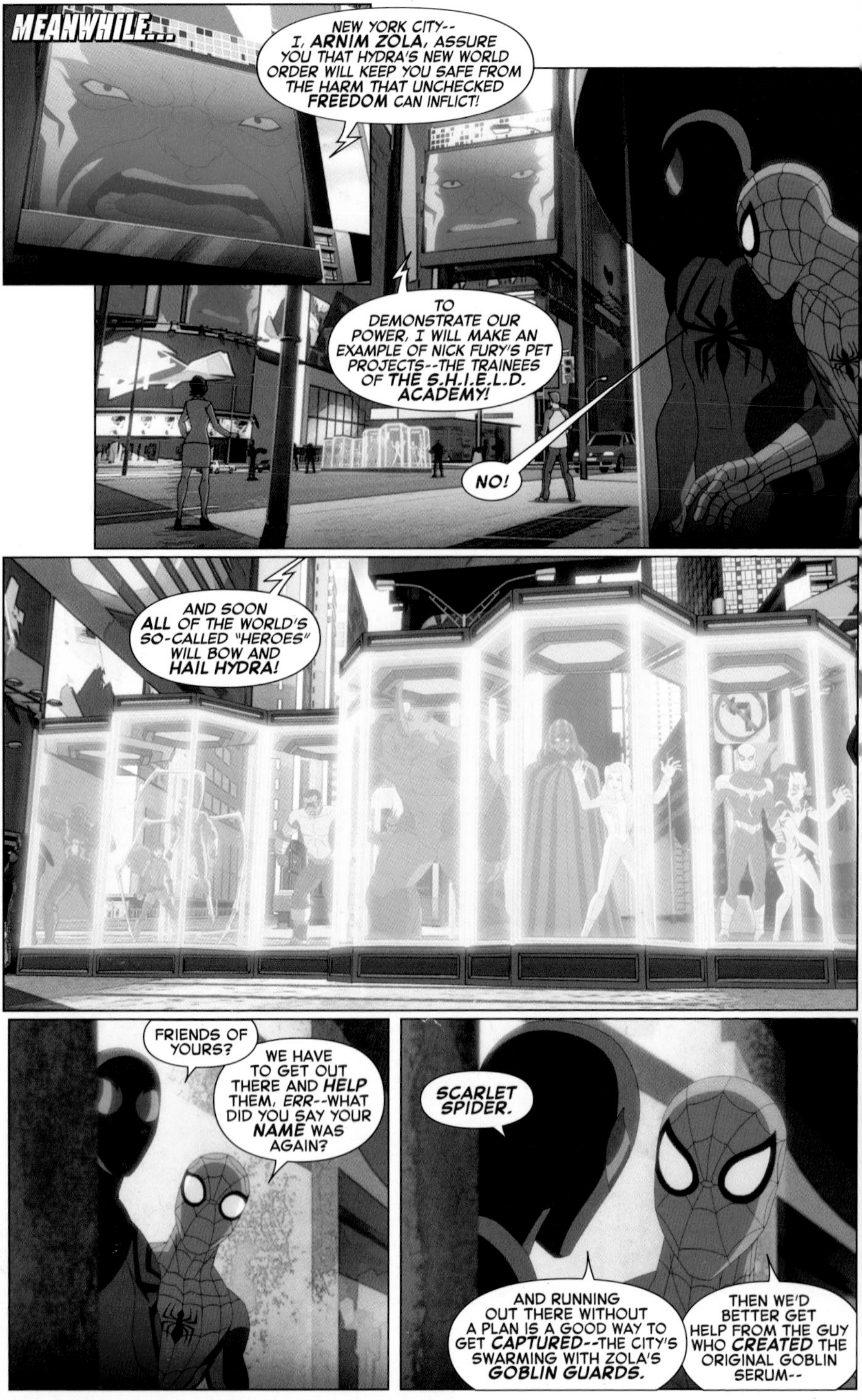
MEANWHILE...
NEW YORK CITY-- I, ARNIM ZOLA, ASSURE YOU THAT HYDRA'S NEW WORLD ORDER WILL KEEP YOU SAFE FROM THE HARM THAT UNCHECKED FREEDOM CAN INFLICT!
TO DEMONSTRATE OUR POWER, I WILL MAKE AN EXAMPLE OF NICK FURY'S PET PROJECTS--THE TRAINEES OF THE S.H.I.E.L.D. ACADEMY!
NO!
AND SOON ALL OF THE WORLD'S SO-CALLED "HEROES" WILL BOW AND HAIL HYDRA!
FRIENDS OF YOURS?
WE HAVE TO GET OUT THERE AND HELP THEM, ERR--WHAT DID YOU SAY YOUR NAME WAS AGAIN?
SCARLET SPIDER.
AND RUNNING OUT THERE WITHOUT A PLAN IS A GOOD WAY TO GET CAPTURED--THE CITY'S SWARMING WITH ZOLA'S GOBLIN GUARDS.
THEN WE'D BETTER GET HELP FROM THE GUY WHO CREATED THE ORIGINAL GOBLIN SERUM--

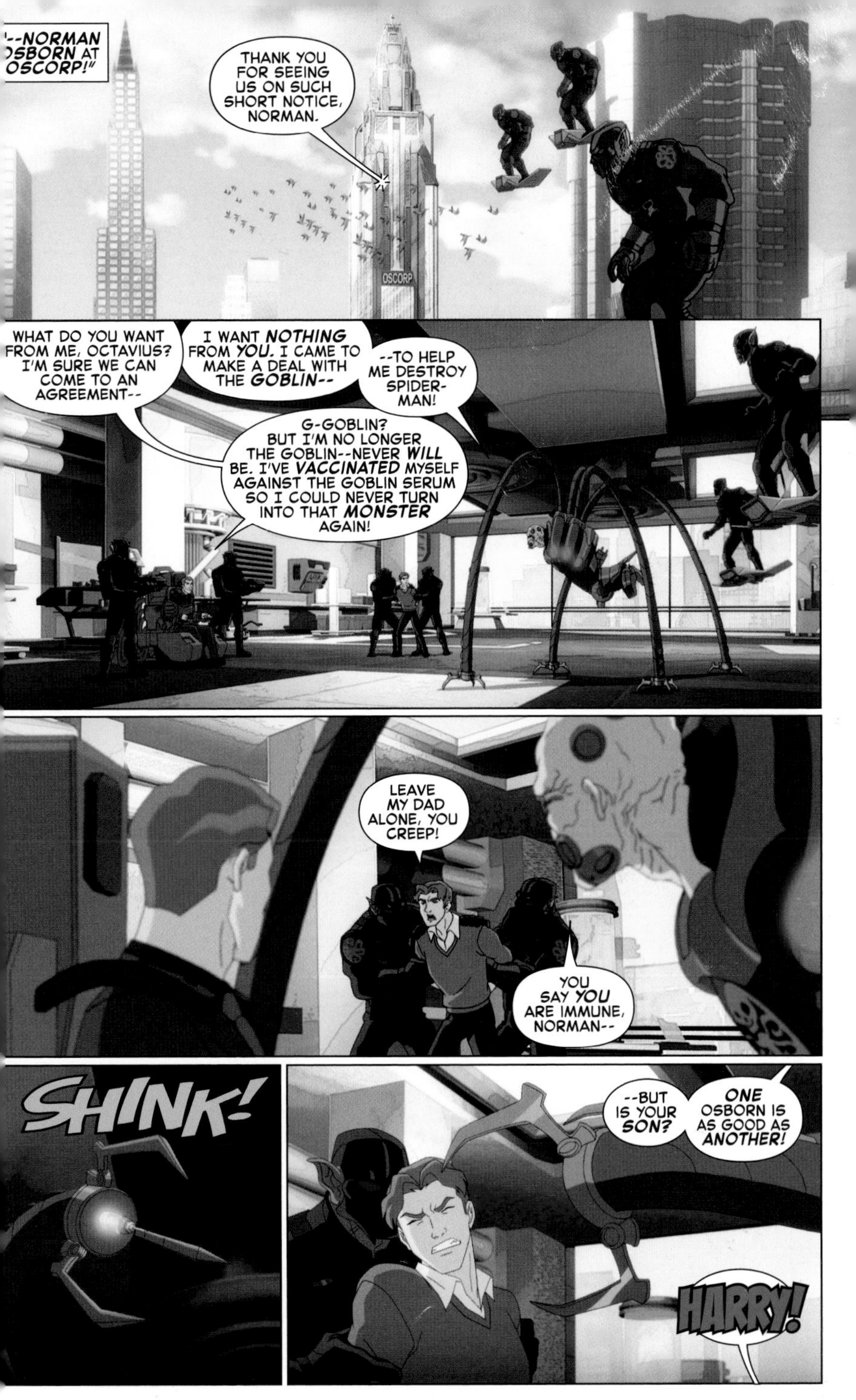
"--NORMAN OSBORN AT OSCORP!"
THANK YOU FOR SEEING US ON SUCH SHORT NOTICE, NORMAN.
OSCORP
WHAT DO YOU WANT FROM ME, OCTAVIUS? I'M SURE WE CAN COME TO AN AGREEMENT--
I WANT NOTHING FROM YOU. I CAME TO MAKE A DEAL WITH THE GOBLIN--
--TO HELP ME DESTROY SPIDER-MAN!
G-GOBLIN? BUT I'M NO LONGER THE GOBLIN--NEVER WILL BE. I'VE VACCINATED MYSELF AGAINST THE GOBLIN SERUM SO I COULD NEVER TURN INTO THAT MONSTER AGAIN!
LEAVE MY DAD ALONE, YOU CREEP!
YOU SAY YOU ARE IMMUNE, NORMAN--
SHINK!
--BUT IS YOUR SON?
ONE OSBORN IS AS GOOD AS ANOTHER!
HARRY!

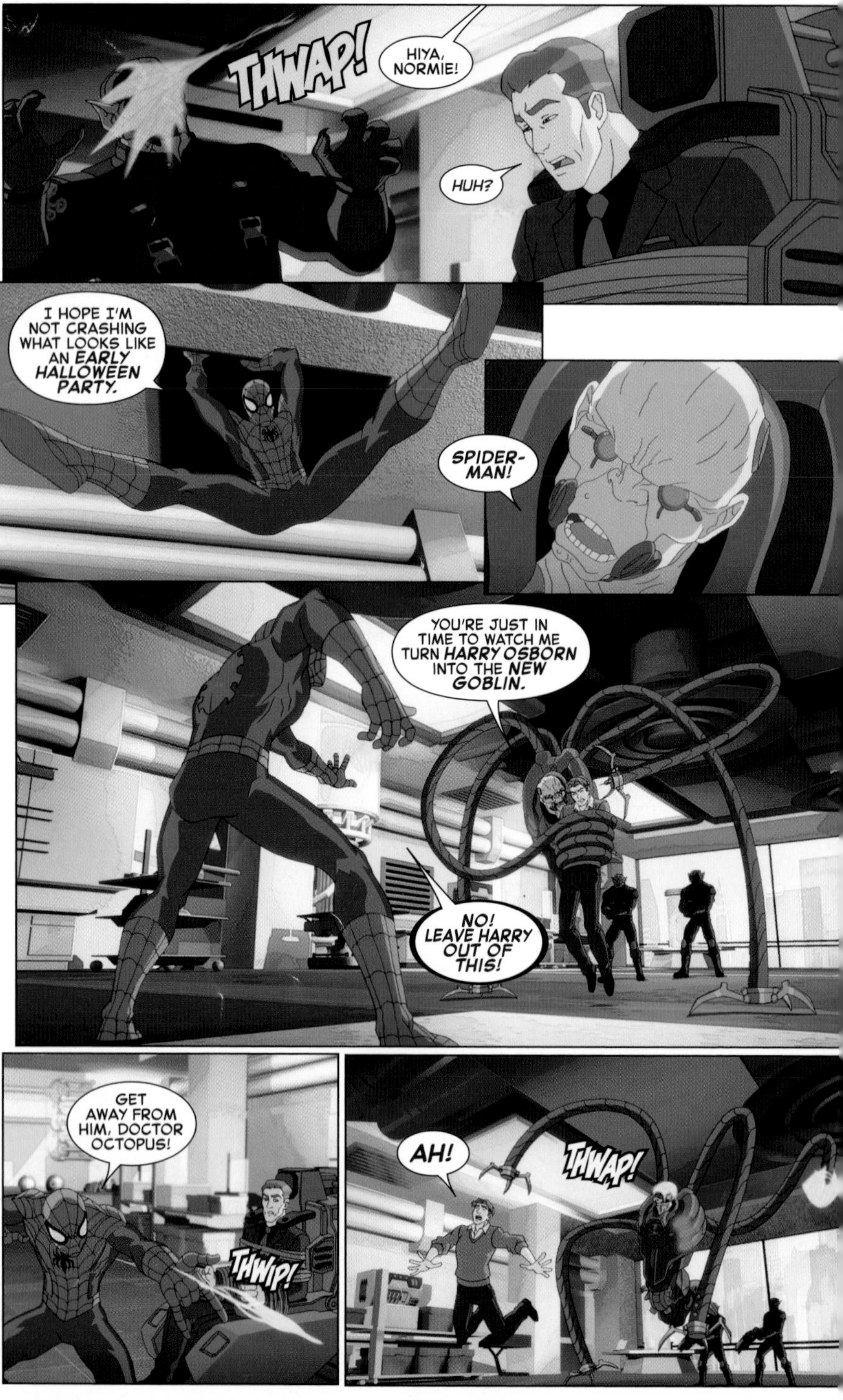
THWAP!
HIYA, NORMIE!
HUH?
I HOPE I'M NOT CRASHING WHAT LOOKS LIKE AN EARLY HALLOWEEN PARTY.
SPIDER-MAN!
YOU'RE JUST IN TIME TO WATCH ME TURN HARRY OSBORN INTO THE NEW GOBLIN.
NO! LEAVE HARRY OUT OF THIS!
GET AWAY FROM HIM, DOCTOR OCTOPUS!
THWIP!
AH!
THWAP!

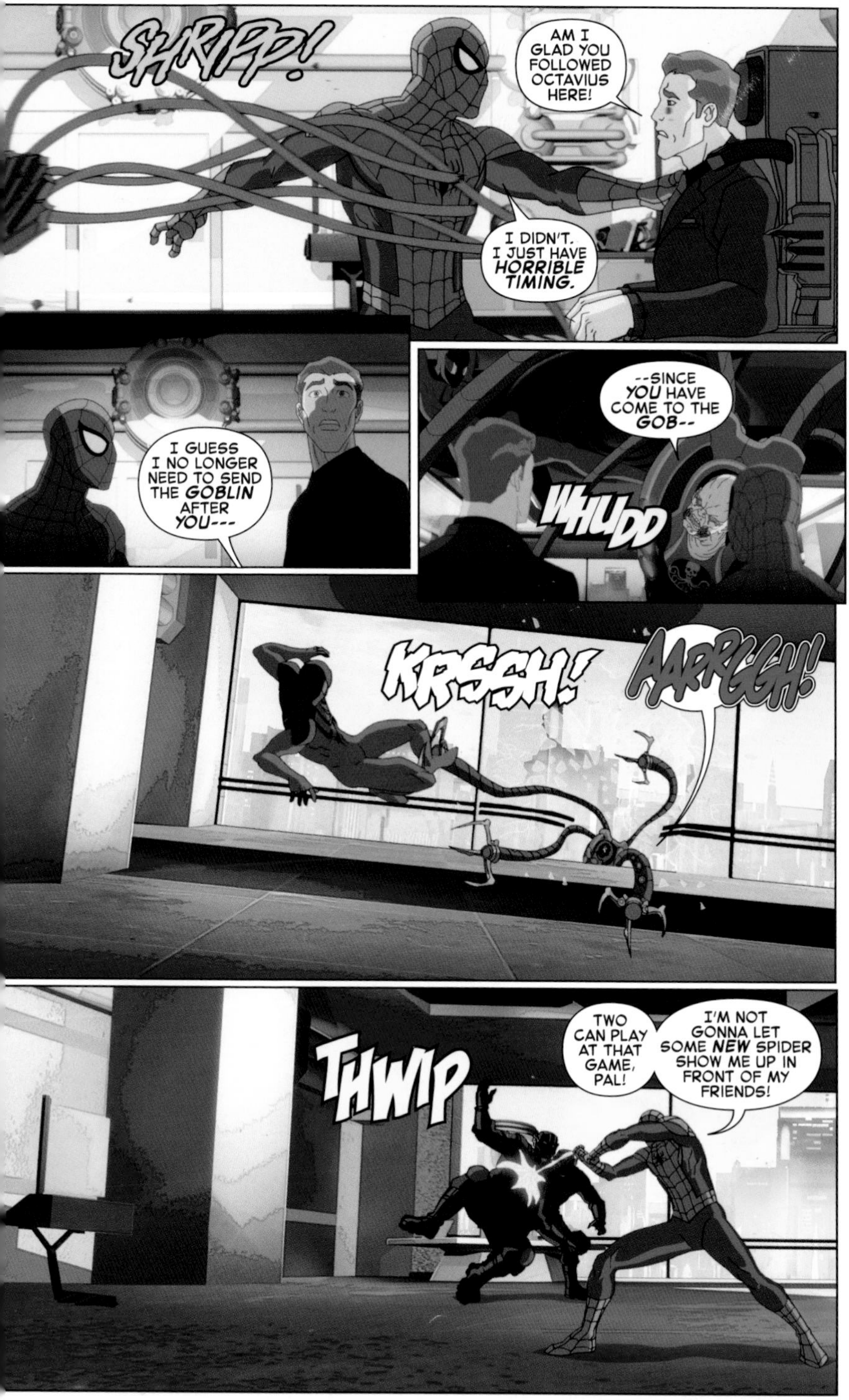
SHRIPP!
AM I GLAD YOU FOLLOWED OCTAVIUS HERE!
I DIDN'T. I JUST HAVE HORRIBLE TIMING.
I GUESS I NO LONGER NEED TO SEND THE GOBLIN AFTER YOU---
--SINCE YOU HAVE COME TO THE GOB--
WHUDD
KRSSH!
AARRGGH!
THWIP
TWO CAN PLAY AT THAT GAME, PAL!
I'M NOT GONNA LET SOME NEW SPIDER SHOW ME UP IN FRONT OF MY FRIENDS!

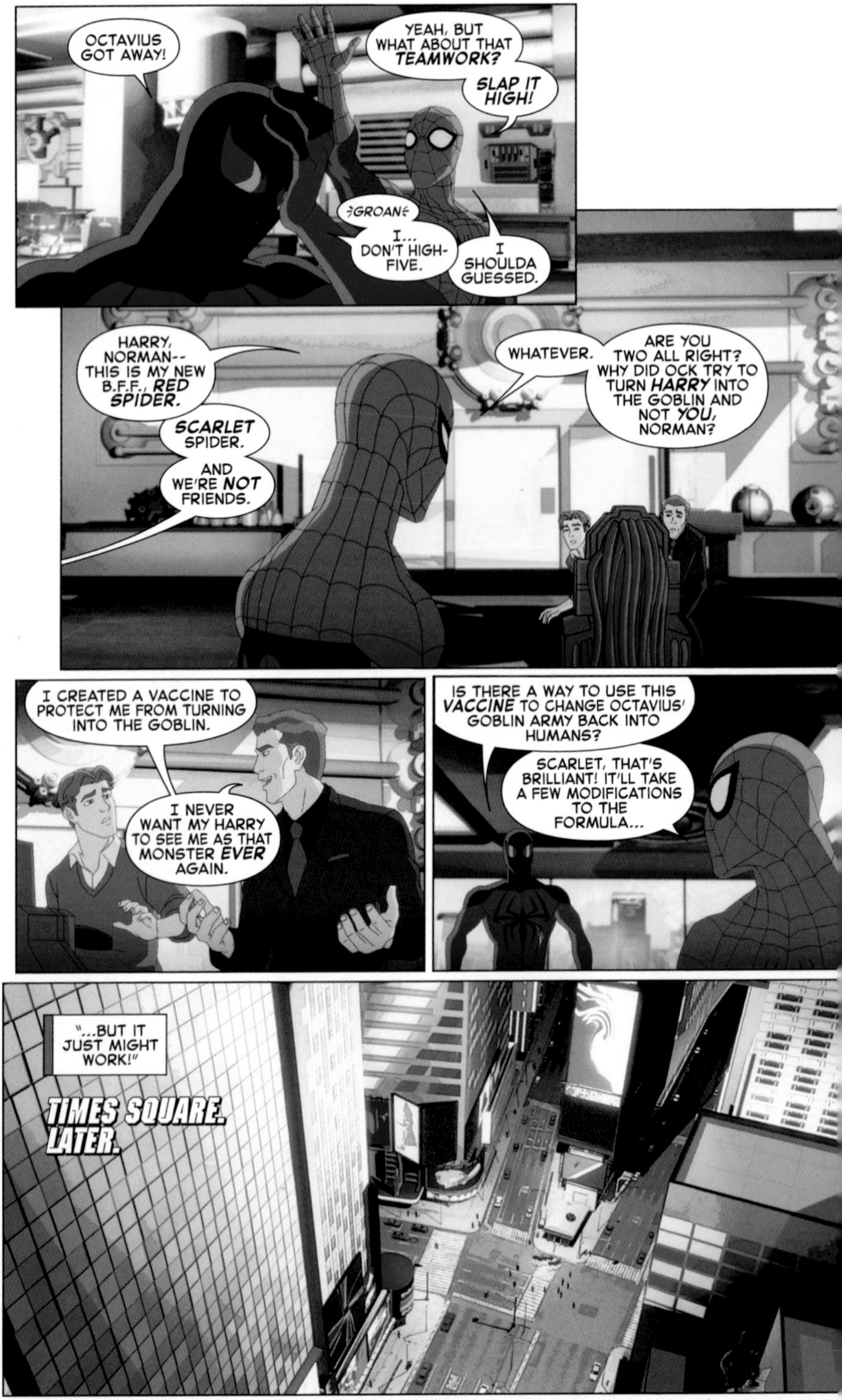
OCTAVIUS GOT AWAY!
YEAH, BUT WHAT ABOUT THAT TEAMWORK?
SLAP IT HIGH!
GROAN
I... DON'T HIGH-FIVE.
I SHOULDA GUESSED.
HARRY, NORMAN-- THIS IS MY NEW B.F.F., RED SPIDER.
SCARLET SPIDER.
AND WE'RE NOT FRIENDS.
WHATEVER.
ARE YOU TWO ALL RIGHT? WHY DID OCK TRY TO TURN HARRY INTO THE GOBLIN AND NOT YOU, NORMAN?
I CREATED A VACCINE TO PROTECT ME FROM TURNING INTO THE GOBLIN.
I NEVER WANT MY HARRY TO SEE ME AS THAT MONSTER EVER AGAIN.
IS THERE A WAY TO USE THIS VACCINE TO CHANGE OCTAVIUS' GOBLIN ARMY BACK INTO HUMANS?
SCARLET, THAT'S BRILLIANT! IT'LL TAKE A FEW MODIFICATIONS TO THE FORMULA...
"...BUT IT JUST MIGHT WORK!"
TIMES SQUARE. LATER.

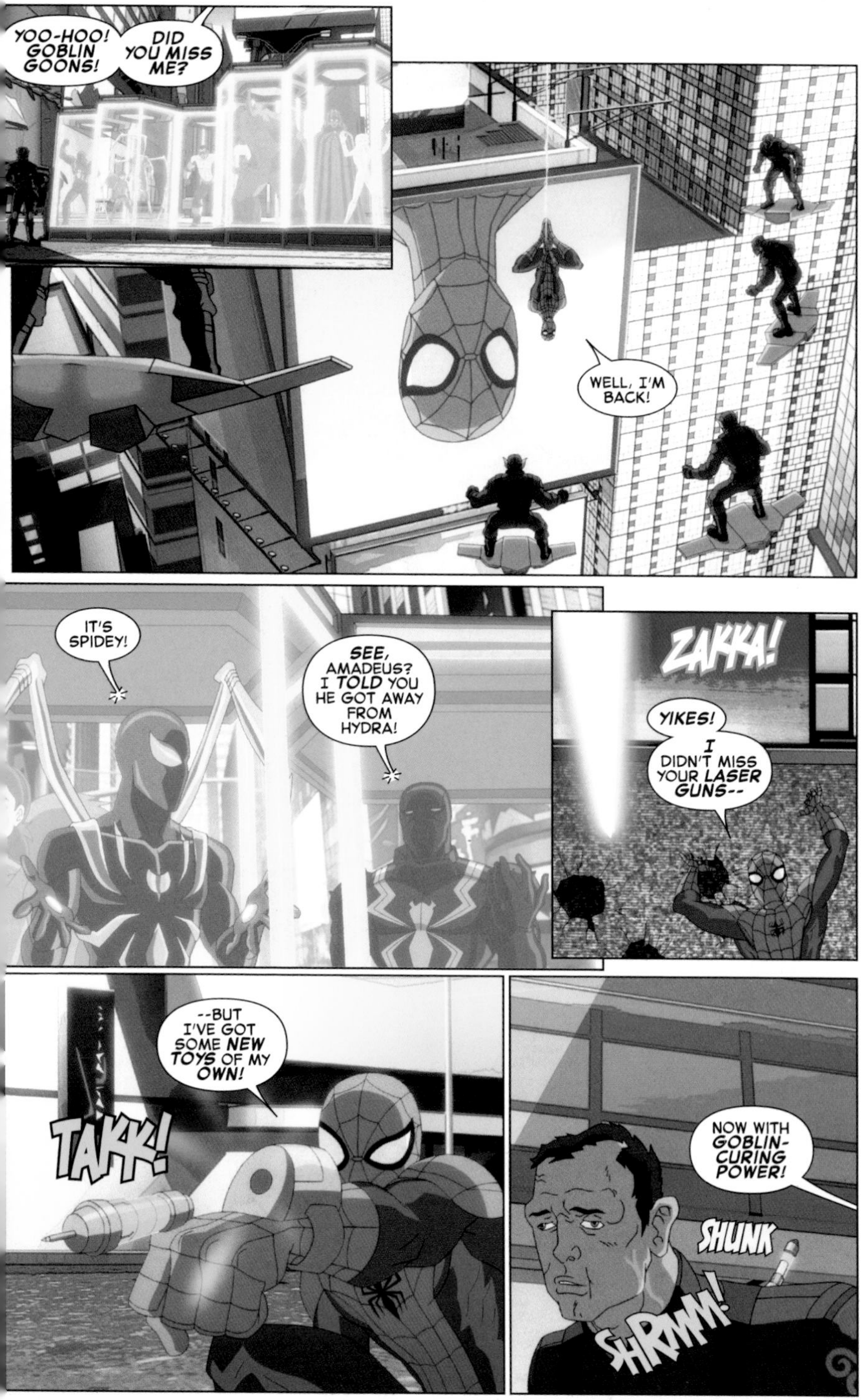
YOO-HOO! GOBLIN GOONS!
DID YOU MISS ME?
WELL, I'M BACK!
IT'S SPIDEY!
SEE, AMADEUS? I TOLD YOU HE GOT AWAY FROM HYDRA!
ZAKKA!
YIKES!
I DIDN'T MISS YOUR LASER GUNS--
--BUT I'VE GOT SOME NEW TOYS OF MY OWN!
TAKK!
NOW WITH GOBLIN-CURING POWER!
SHUNK
SHRMM!

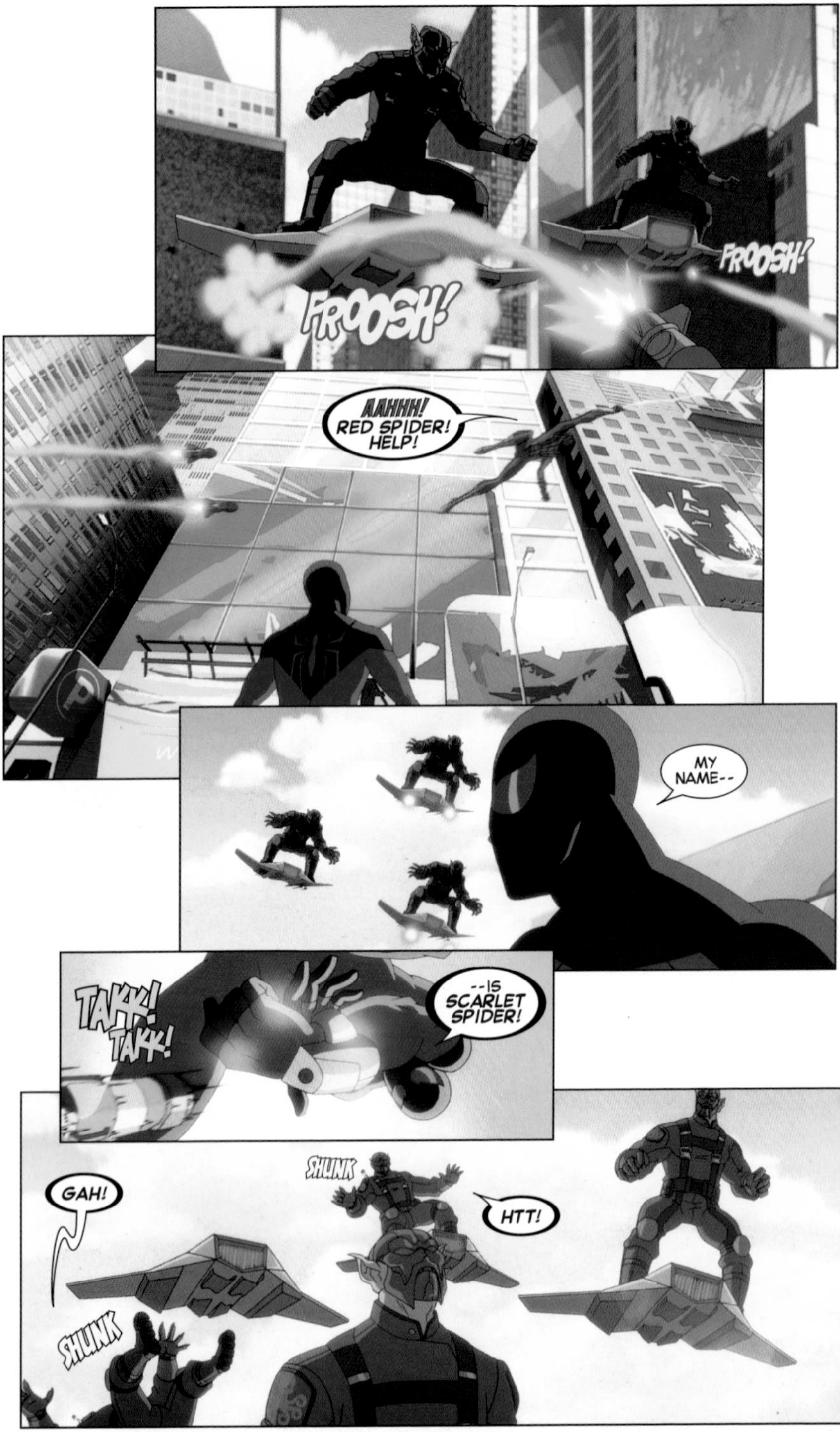
FROOSH!
FROOSH!
AAHHH! RED SPIDER! HELP!
MY NAME--
TAKK! TAKK!
--IS SCARLET SPIDER!
SHUNK
GAH!
HTT!
SHUNK

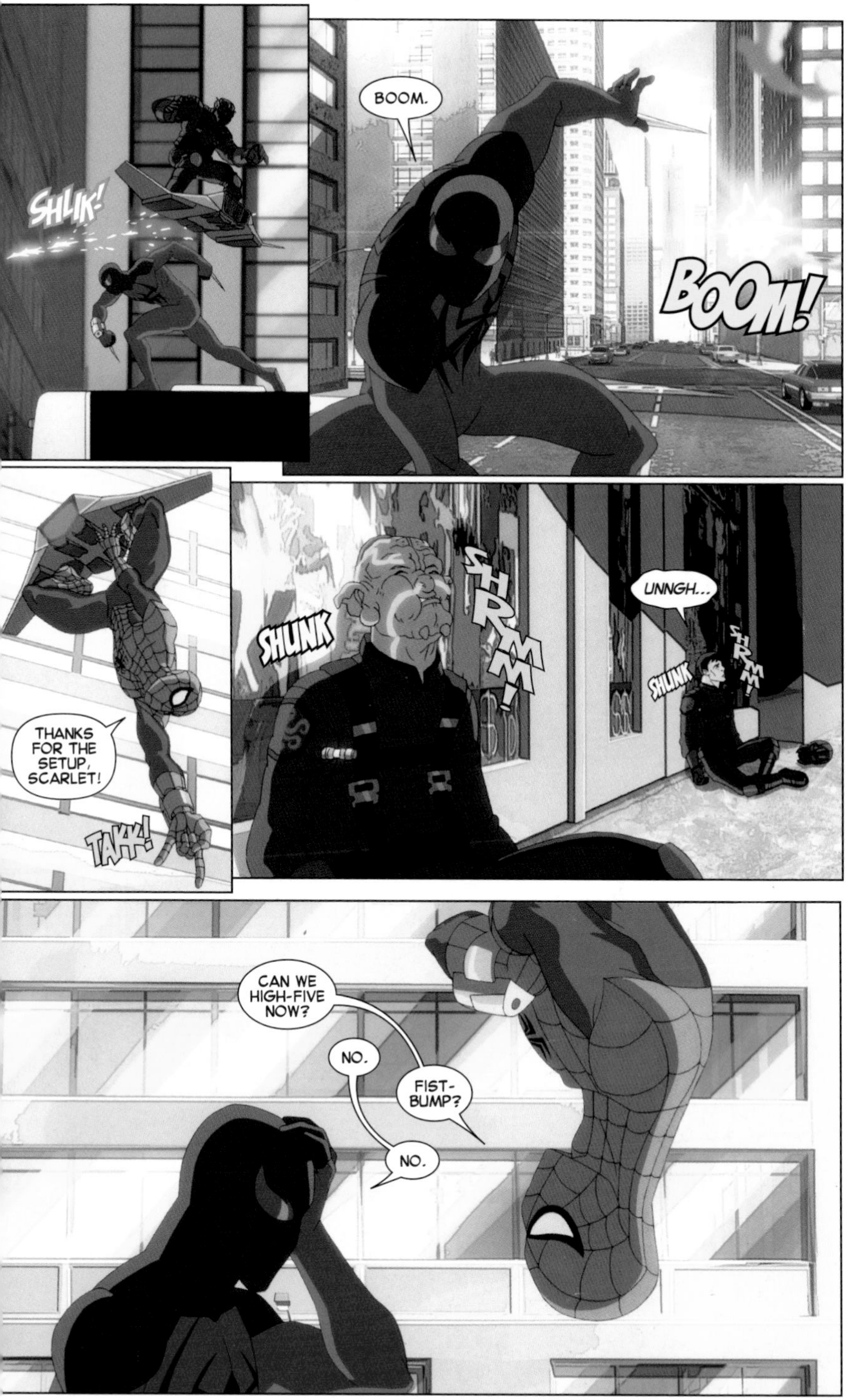
SHLIK!
BOOM.
BOOM!
THANKS FOR THE SETUP, SCARLET!
TAKK!
SHUNK
SHRMM!
UNNGH...
SHUNK
SHRMM!
CAN WE HIGH-FIVE NOW?
NO.
FIST-BUMP?
NO.

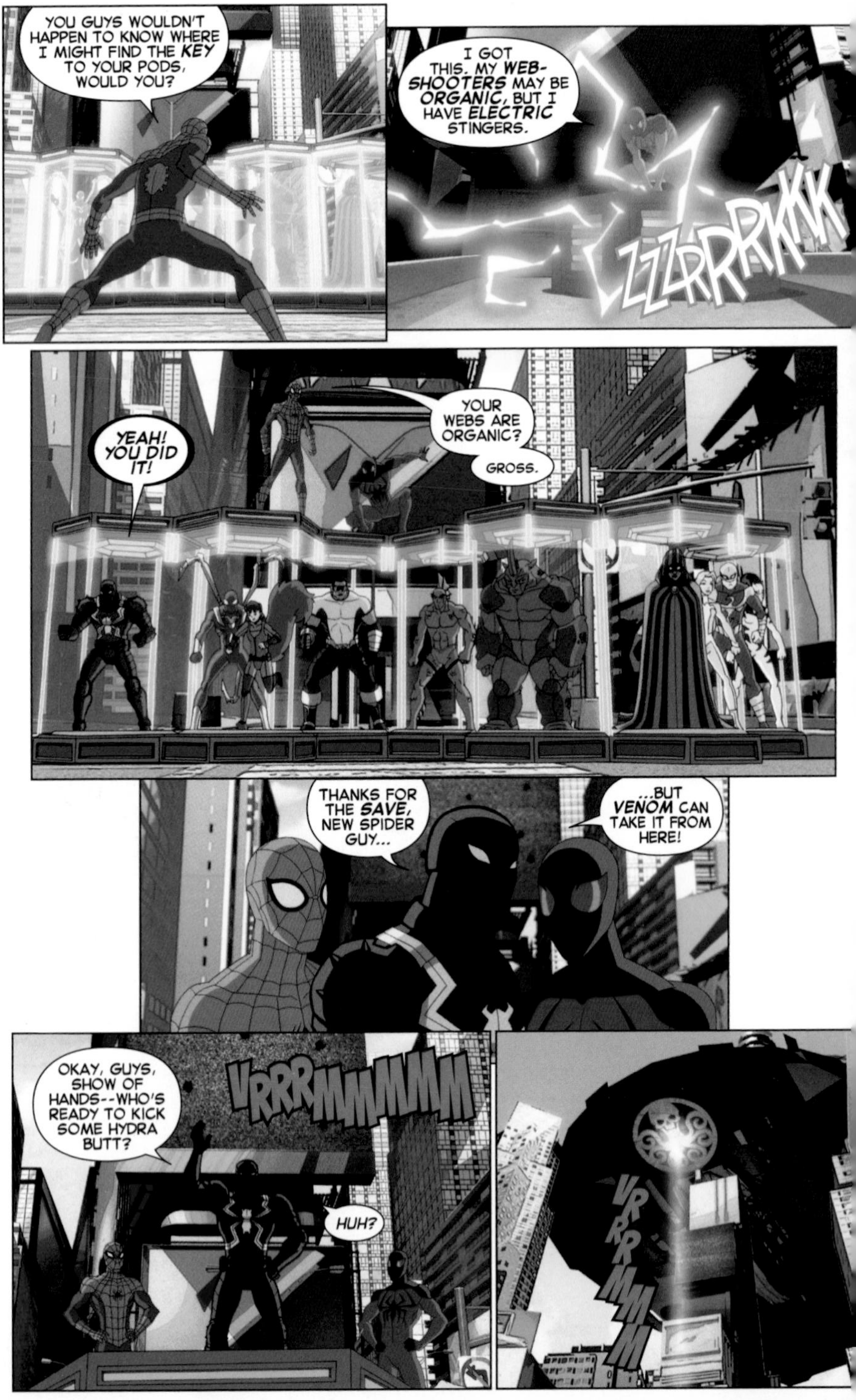
YOU GUYS WOULDN'T HAPPEN TO KNOW WHERE I MIGHT FIND THE KEY TO YOUR PODS, WOULD YOU?
I GOT THIS. MY WEB-SHOOTERS MAY BE ORGANIC, BUT I HAVE ELECTRIC STINGERS.
ZZZRRRKKK
YEAH! YOU DID IT!
YOUR WEBS ARE ORGANIC?
GROSS.
THANKS FOR THE SAVE, NEW SPIDER GUY...
...BUT VENOM CAN TAKE IT FROM HERE!
OKAY, GUYS, SHOW OF HANDS--WHO'S READY TO KICK SOME HYDRA BUTT?
VRRRMMMMMM
HUH?
VRRRMMMM

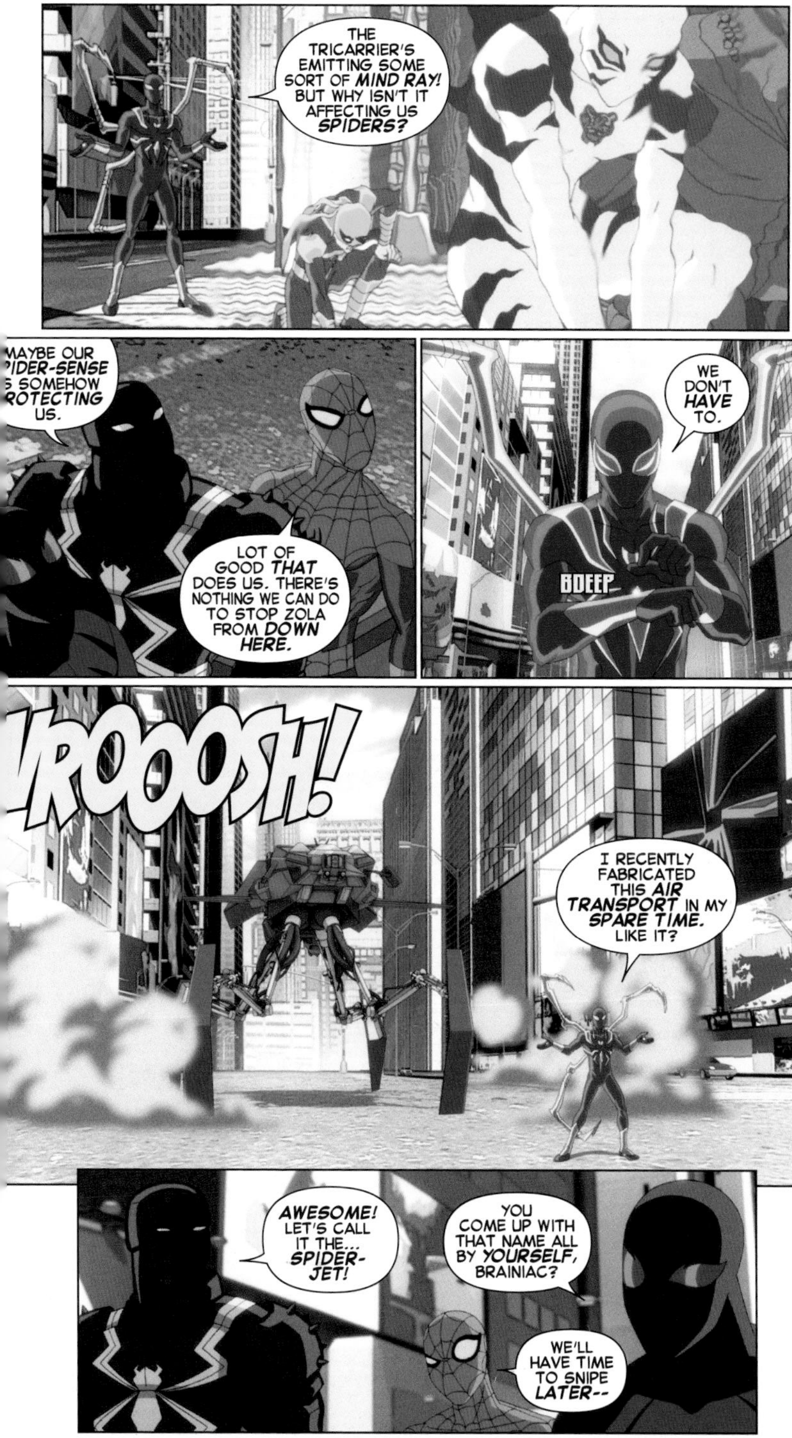

THE TRICARRIER'S EMITTING SOME SORT OF MIND RAY! BUT WHY ISN'T IT AFFECTING US SPIDERS?
MAYBE OUR SPIDER-SENSE IS SOMEHOW PROTECTING US.
LOT OF GOOD THAT DOES US. THERE'S NOTHING WE CAN DO TO STOP ZOLA FROM DOWN HERE.
WE DON'T HAVE TO.
BDEEP
VROOOSH!
I RECENTLY FABRICATED THIS AIR TRANSPORT IN MY SPARE TIME. LIKE IT?
AWESOME! LET'S CALL IT THE... SPIDER-JET!
YOU COME UP WITH THAT NAME ALL BY YOURSELF, BRAINIAC?
WE'LL HAVE TIME TO SNIPE LATER--

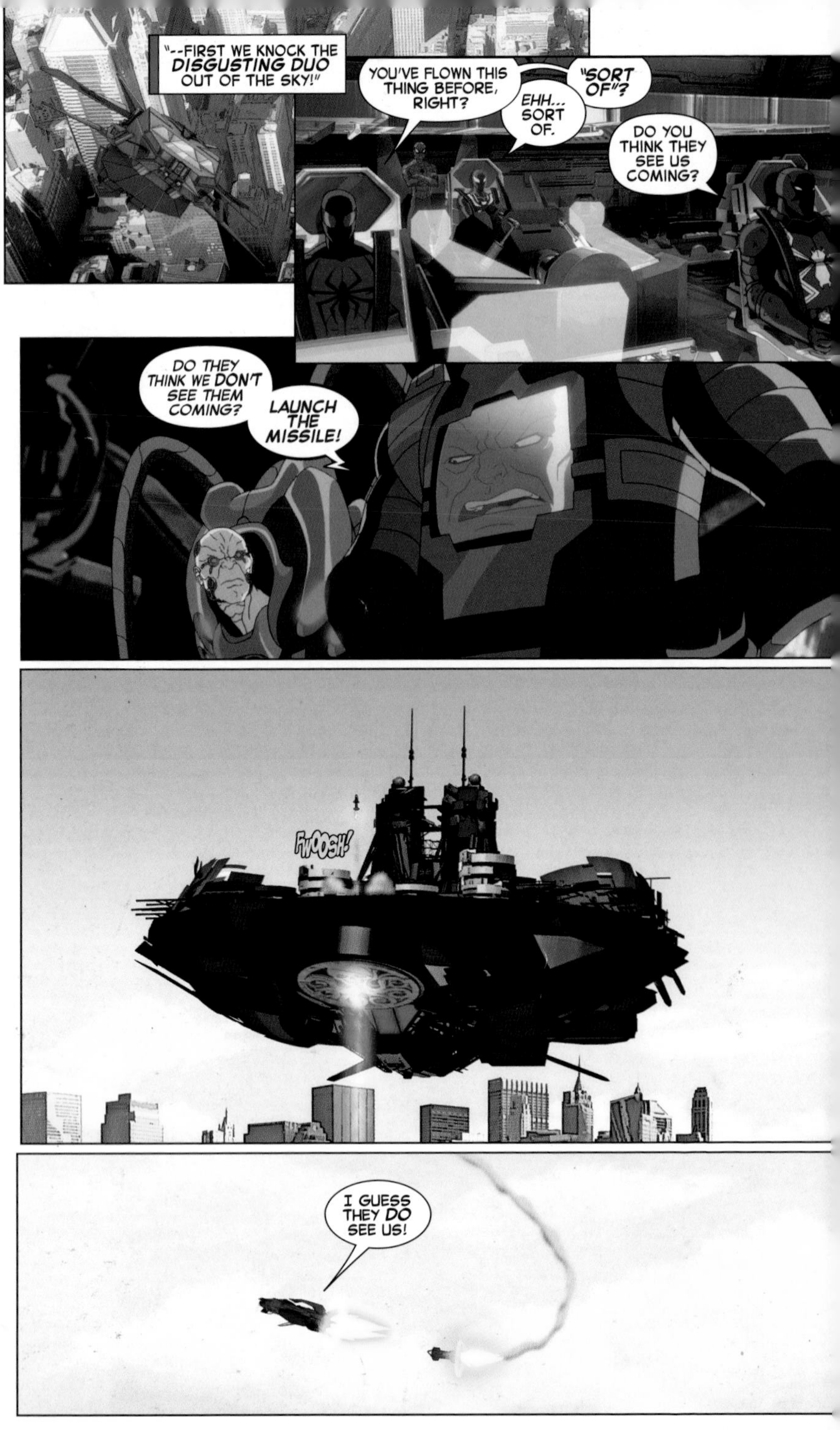
"--FIRST WE KNOCK THE DISGUSTING DUO OUT OF THE SKY!"
YOU'VE FLOWN THIS THING BEFORE, RIGHT?
EHH... SORT OF.
"SORT OF"?
DO YOU THINK THEY SEE US COMING?
DO THEY THINK WE DON'T SEE THEM COMING?
LAUNCH THE MISSILE!
FWOOSH!
I GUESS THEY DO SEE US!

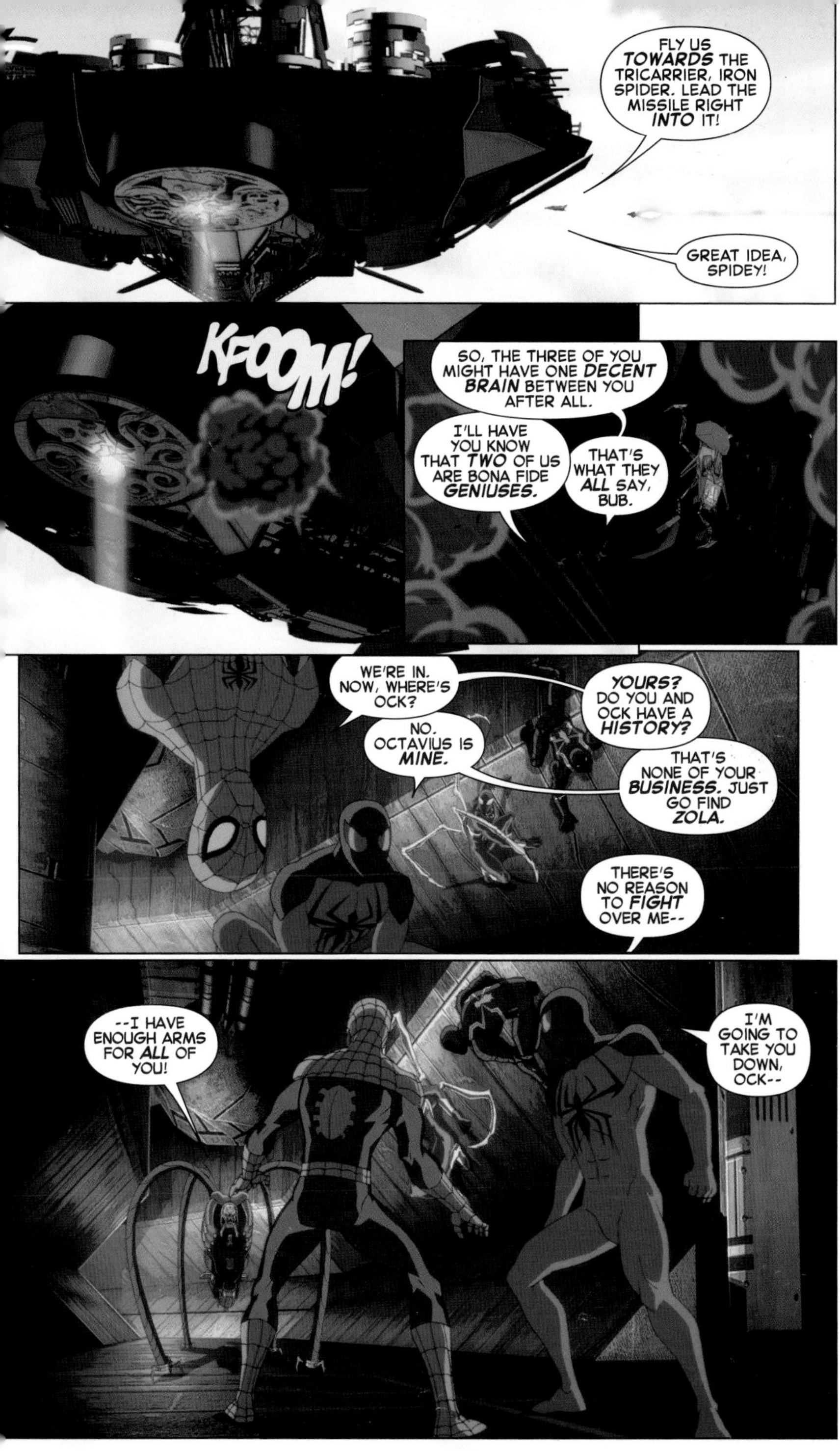
FLY US TOWARDS THE TRICARRIER, IRON SPIDER. LEAD THE MISSILE RIGHT INTO IT!
GREAT IDEA, SPIDEY!
KFOOM!
SO, THE THREE OF YOU MIGHT HAVE ONE DECENT BRAIN BETWEEN YOU AFTER ALL.
I'LL HAVE YOU KNOW THAT TWO OF US ARE BONA FIDE GENIUSES.
THAT'S WHAT THEY ALL SAY, BUB.
WE'RE IN. NOW, WHERE'S OCK?
NO. OCTAVIUS IS MINE.
YOURS? DO YOU AND OCK HAVE A HISTORY?
THAT'S NONE OF YOUR BUSINESS. JUST GO FIND ZOLA.
THERE'S NO REASON TO FIGHT OVER ME--
--I HAVE ENOUGH ARMS FOR ALL OF YOU!
I'M GOING TO TAKE YOU DOWN, OCK--

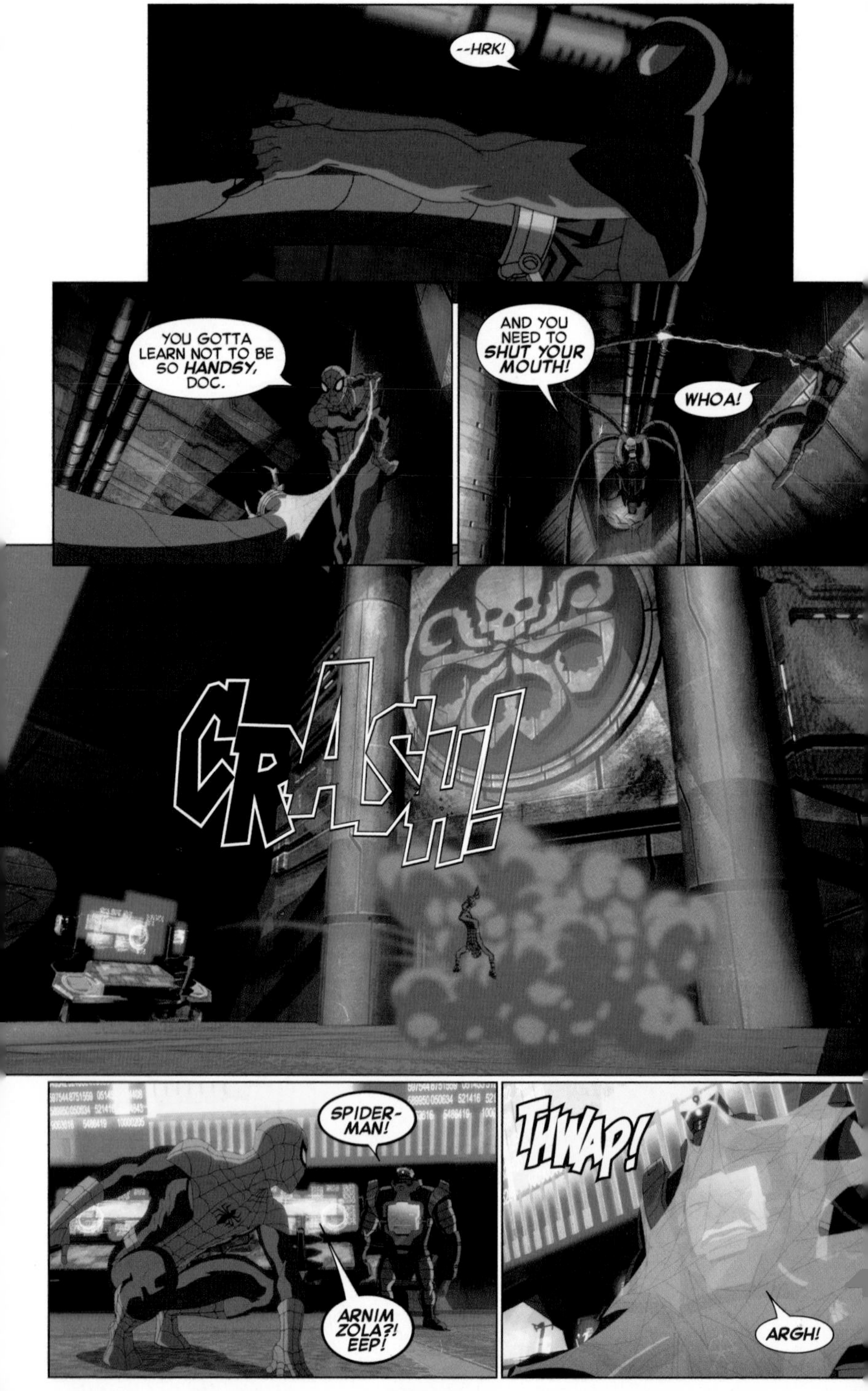
--HRK!
YOU GOTTA LEARN NOT TO BE SO HANDSY, DOC.
AND YOU NEED TO SHUT YOUR MOUTH!
WHOA!
CRASH!
SPIDER-MAN!
ARNIM ZOLA?! EEP!
THWAP!
ARGH!

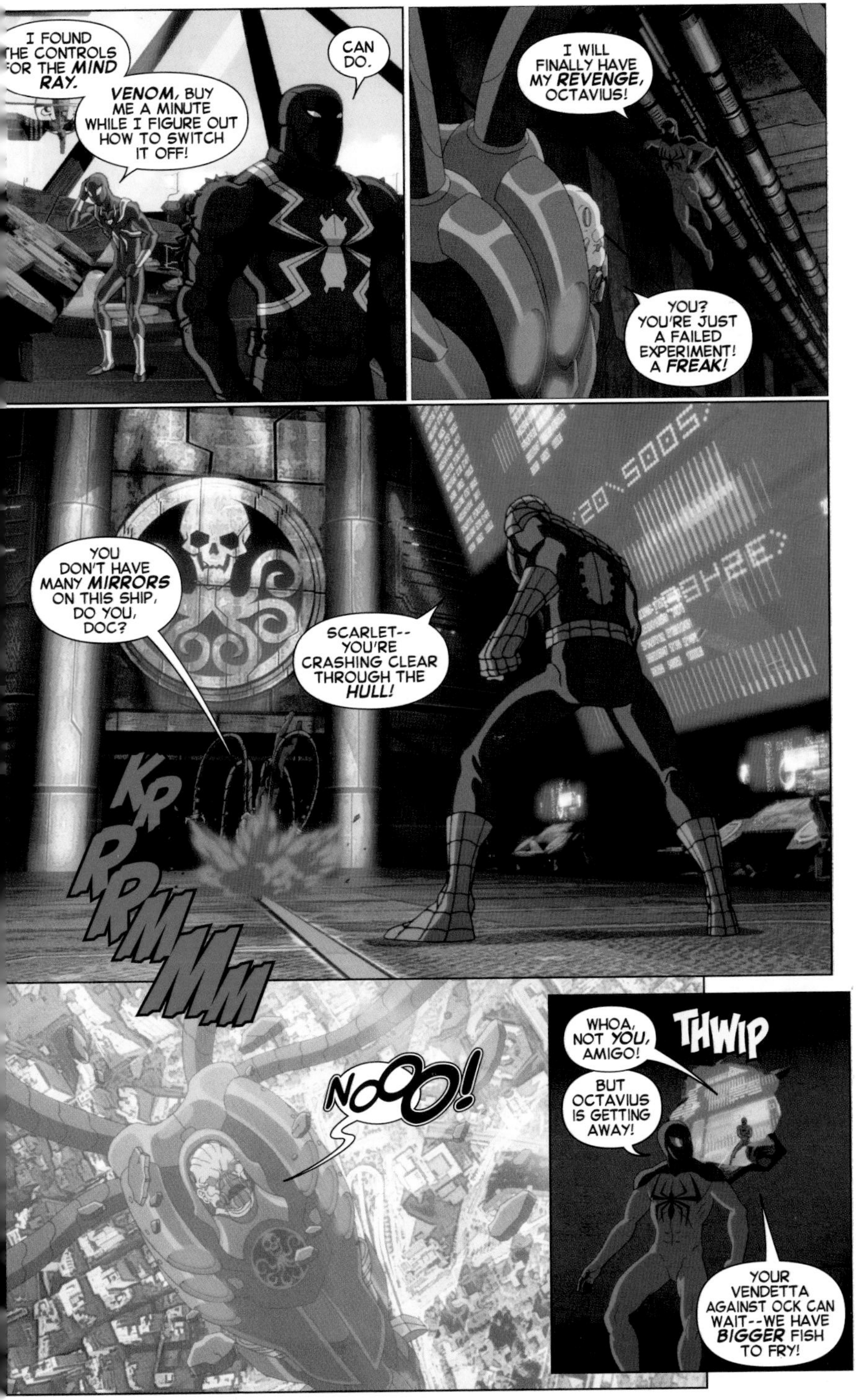
I FOUND THE CONTROLS FOR THE MIND RAY.
VENOM, BUY ME A MINUTE WHILE I FIGURE OUT HOW TO SWITCH IT OFF!
CAN DO.
I WILL FINALLY HAVE MY REVENGE, OCTAVIUS!
YOU? YOU'RE JUST A FAILED EXPERIMENT! A FREAK!
YOU DON'T HAVE MANY MIRRORS ON THIS SHIP, DO YOU, DOC?
SCARLET-- YOU'RE CRASHING CLEAR THROUGH THE HULL!
KRRRMMMM
NOOO!
WHOA, NOT YOU, AMIGO!
THWIP
BUT OCTAVIUS IS GETTING AWAY!
YOUR VENDETTA AGAINST OCK CAN WAIT--WE HAVE BIGGER FISH TO FRY!

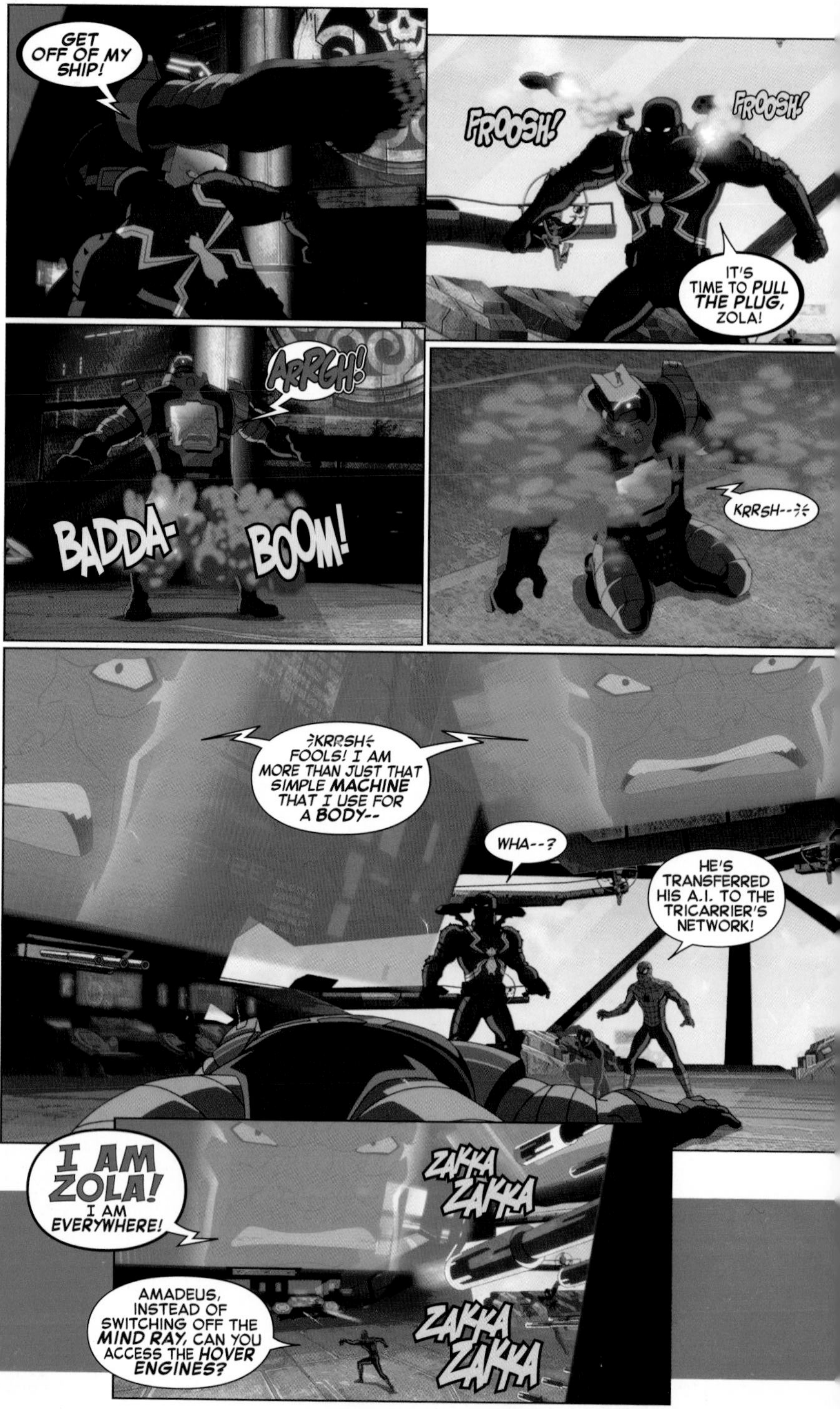
GET OFF OF MY SHIP!
FROOSH!
FROOSH!
IT'S TIME TO PULL THE PLUG, ZOLA!
ARRGH!
BADDA-
BOOM!
KRRSH--
KRRSH FOOLS! I AM MORE THAN JUST THAT SIMPLE MACHINE THAT I USE FOR A BODY--
WHA--?
HE'S TRANSFERRED HIS A.I. TO THE TRICARRIER'S NETWORK!
I AM ZOLA! I AM EVERYWHERE!
ZAKKA ZAKKA
AMADEUS, INSTEAD OF SWITCHING OFF THE MIND RAY, CAN YOU ACCESS THE HOVER ENGINES?
ZAKKA ZAKKA

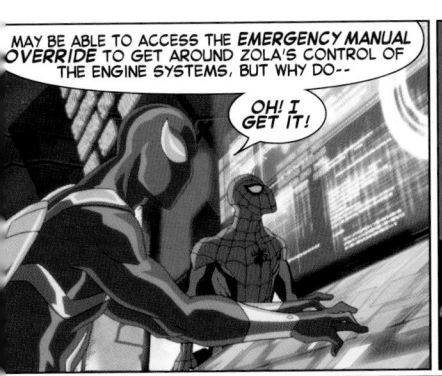

MAY BE ABLE TO ACCESS THE *EMERGENCY MANUAL OVERRIDE* TO GET AROUND ZOLA'S CONTROL OF THE ENGINE SYSTEMS, BUT WHY DO--

OH! I GET IT!

WHAT ARE YOU DOING?!

IF THE TRICARRIER IS YOUR NEW BODY, THEN IT'S ALSO YOUR PRISON--

I'M SETTING A COURSE FOR *SATURN*--

SHRAP!

AH!

IRON *SPIDER!* WHAT--

KRAVEN THE HUNTER!

WHAT ARE YOU DOING HERE?!

ZZZRRRKKK!

AAHHH!

I WAS HERE *ALL* ALONG...

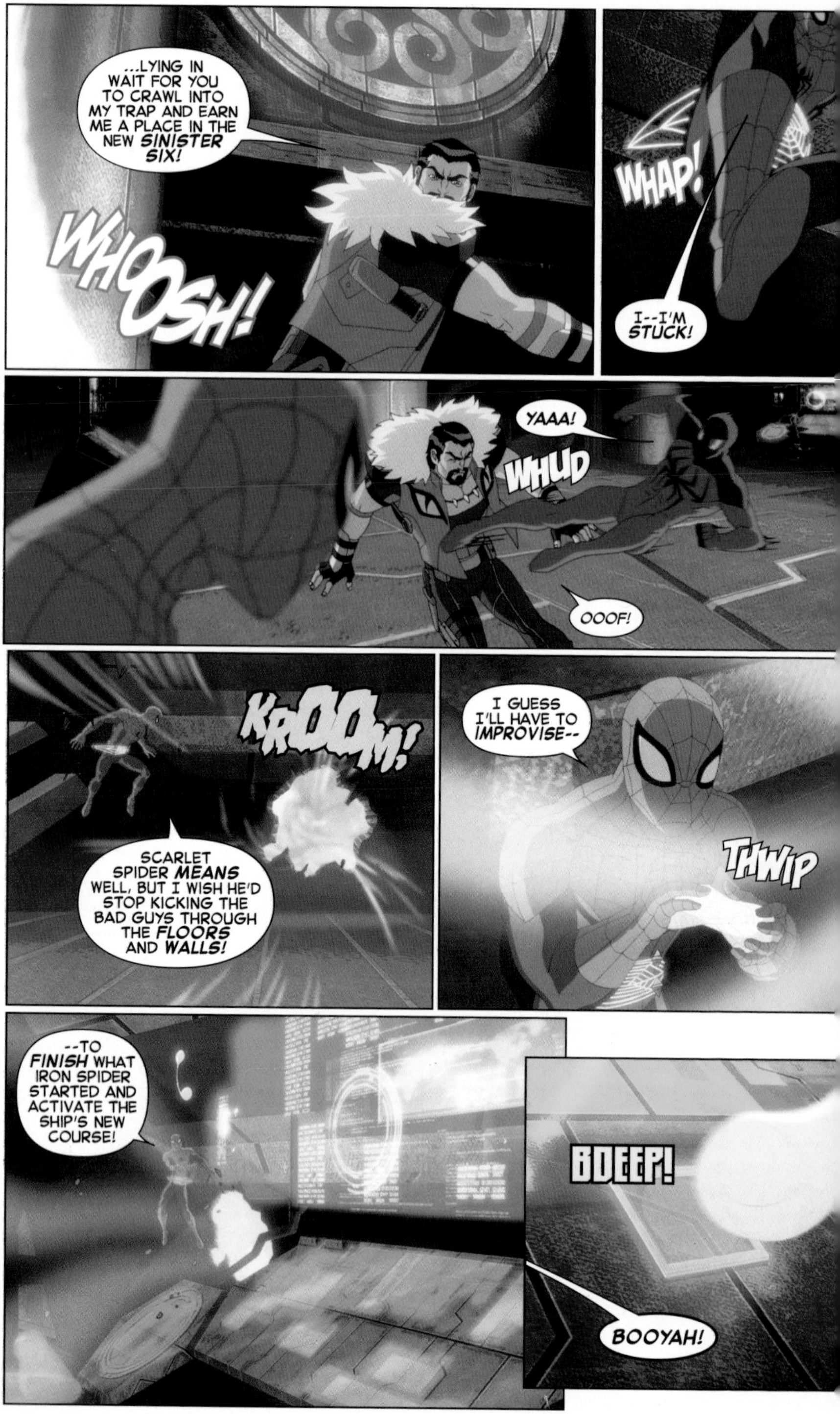
...LYING IN WAIT FOR YOU TO CRAWL INTO MY TRAP AND EARN ME A PLACE IN THE NEW SINISTER SIX!
WHOOOSH!
WHAP!
I--I'M STUCK!
YAAA!
WHUD
OOOF!
KROOOM!
SCARLET SPIDER MEANS WELL, BUT I WISH HE'D STOP KICKING THE BAD GUYS THROUGH THE FLOORS AND WALLS!
I GUESS I'LL HAVE TO IMPROVISE--
THWIP
--TO FINISH WHAT IRON SPIDER STARTED AND ACTIVATE THE SHIP'S NEW COURSE!
BDEEP!
BOOYAH!

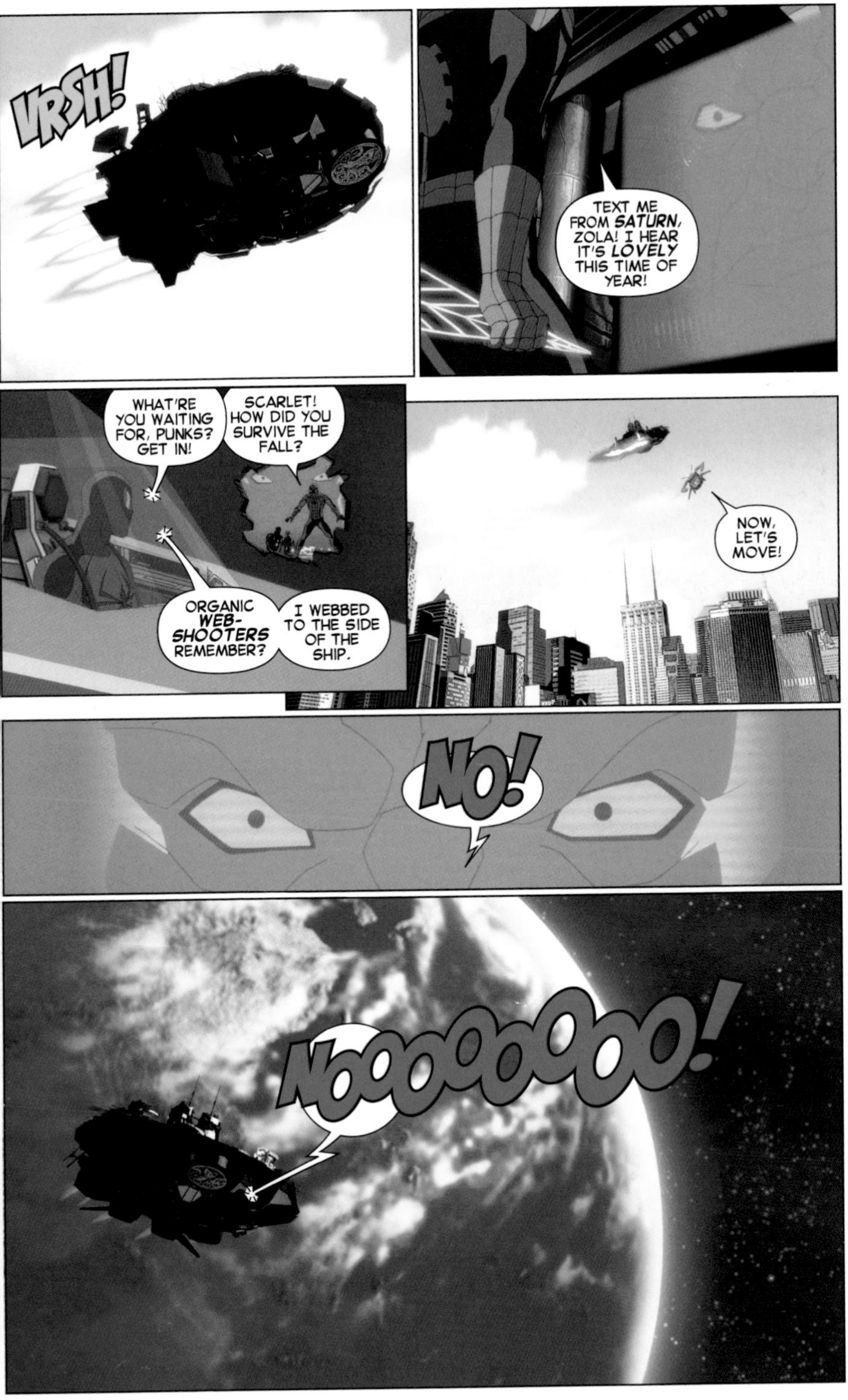
VRSH!
TEXT ME FROM SATURN, ZOLA! I HEAR IT'S LOVELY THIS TIME OF YEAR!
WHAT'RE YOU WAITING FOR, PUNKS? GET IN!
SCARLET! HOW DID YOU SURVIVE THE FALL?
ORGANIC WEB-SHOOTERS REMEMBER?
I WEBBED TO THE SIDE OF THE SHIP.
NOW, LET'S MOVE!
NO!
NOOOOOOOO!

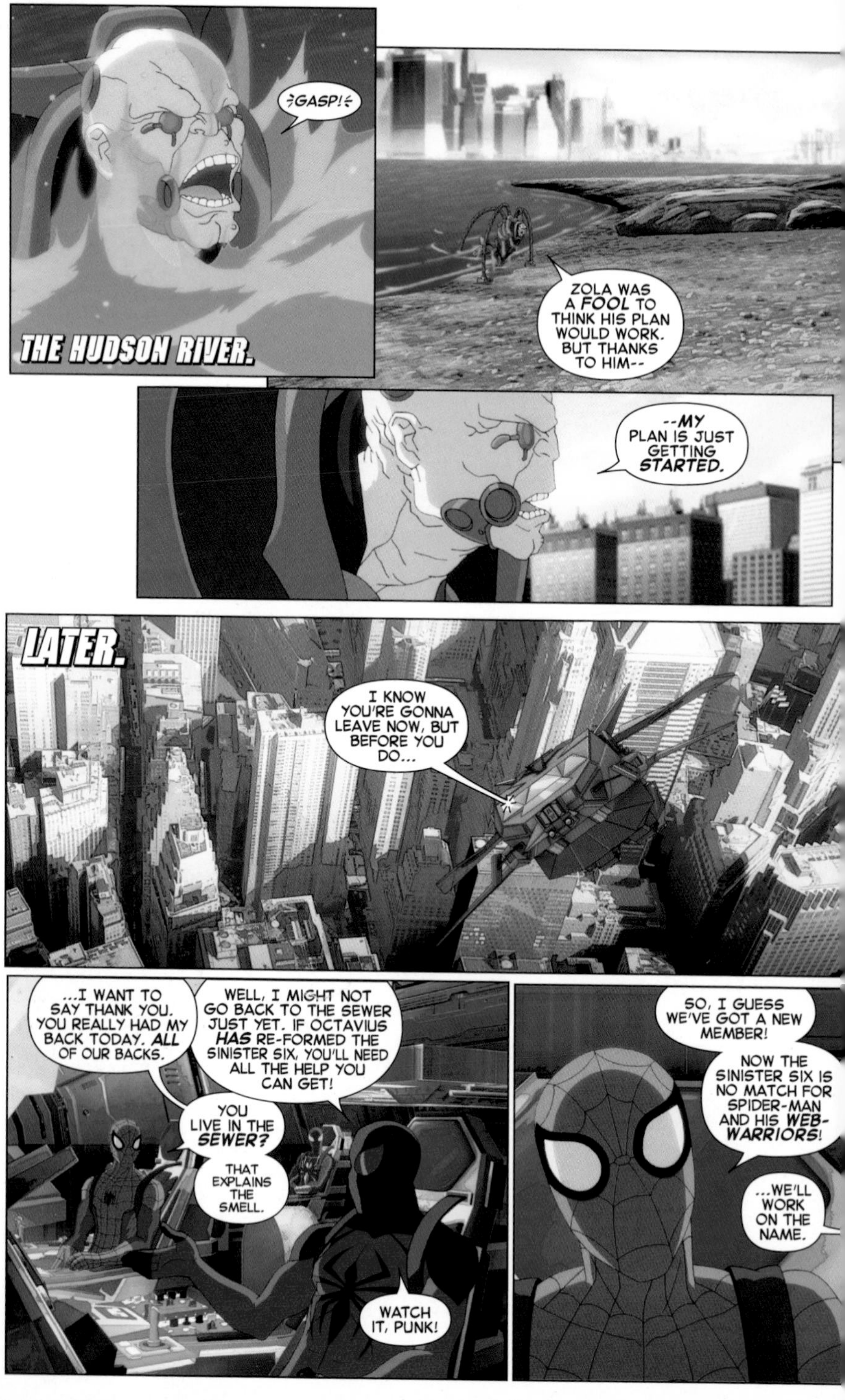

THE HUDSON RIVER.
GASP!
ZOLA WAS A FOOL TO THINK HIS PLAN WOULD WORK. BUT THANKS TO HIM--
--MY PLAN IS JUST GETTING STARTED.
LATER.
I KNOW YOU'RE GONNA LEAVE NOW, BUT BEFORE YOU DO...
...I WANT TO SAY THANK YOU. YOU REALLY HAD MY BACK TODAY. ALL OF OUR BACKS.
WELL, I MIGHT NOT GO BACK TO THE SEWER JUST YET. IF OCTAVIUS HAS RE-FORMED THE SINISTER SIX, YOU'LL NEED ALL THE HELP YOU CAN GET!
YOU LIVE IN THE SEWER?
THAT EXPLAINS THE SMELL.
WATCH IT, PUNK!
SO, I GUESS WE'VE GOT A NEW MEMBER!
NOW THE SINISTER SIX IS NO MATCH FOR SPIDER-MAN AND HIS WEB-WARRIORS!
...WE'LL WORK ON THE NAME.

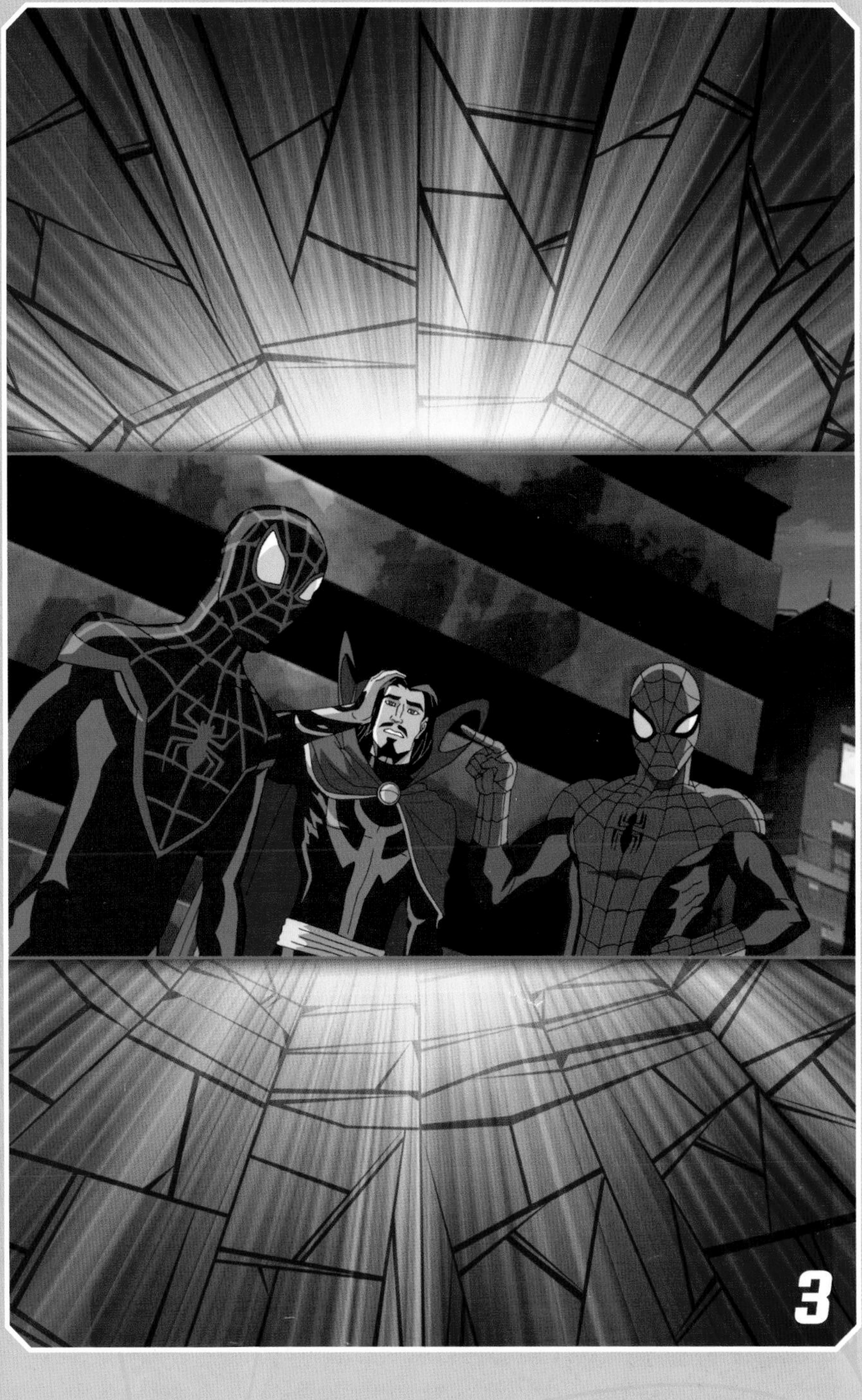

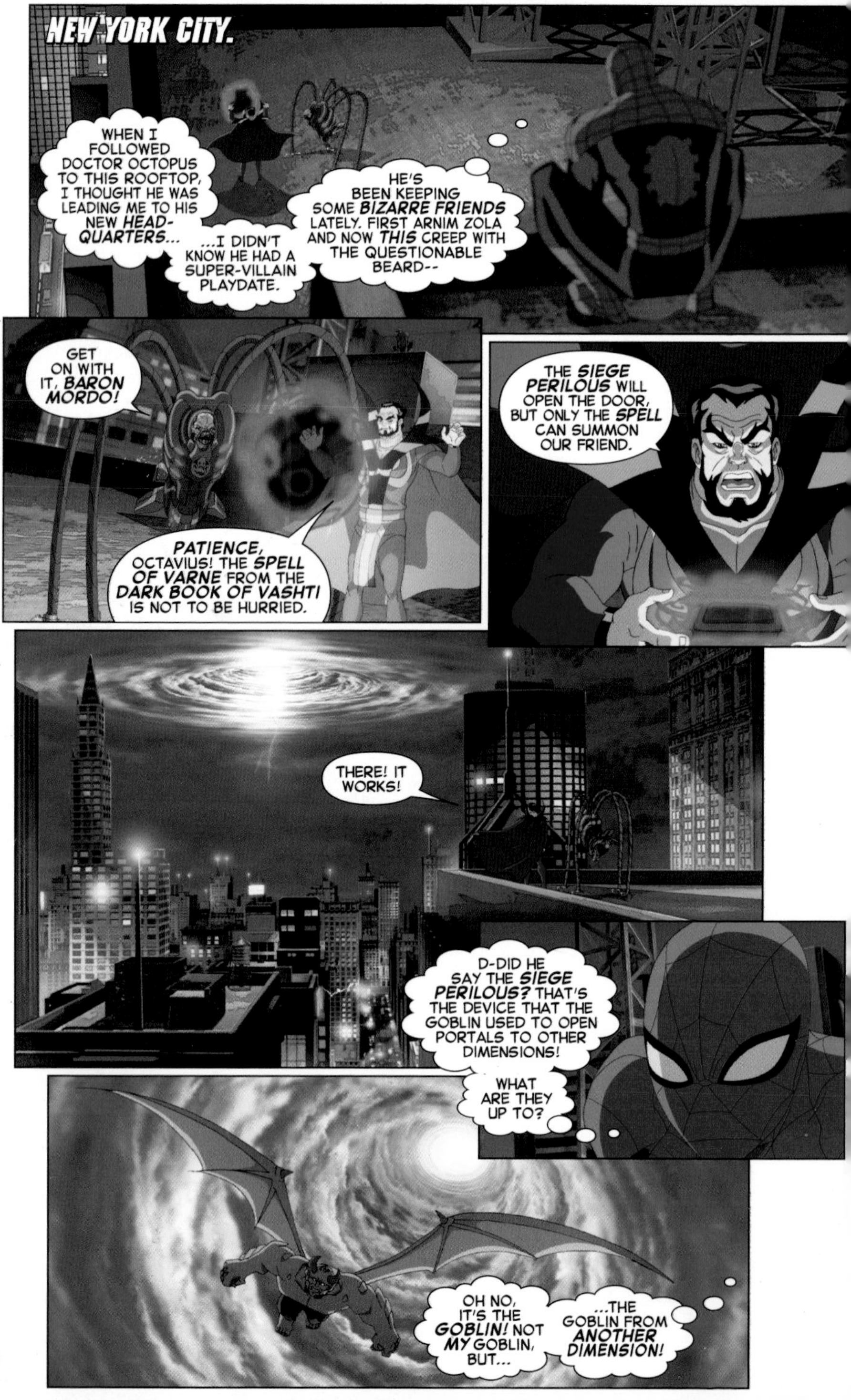
NEW YORK CITY.
WHEN I FOLLOWED DOCTOR OCTOPUS TO THIS ROOFTOP, I THOUGHT HE WAS LEADING ME TO HIS NEW HEAD-QUARTERS...
...I DIDN'T KNOW HE HAD A SUPER-VILLAIN PLAYDATE.
HE'S BEEN KEEPING SOME BIZARRE FRIENDS LATELY. FIRST ARNIM ZOLA AND NOW THIS CREEP WITH THE QUESTIONABLE BEARD--
GET ON WITH IT, BARON MORDO!
PATIENCE, OCTAVIUS! THE SPELL OF VARNE FROM THE DARK BOOK OF VASHTI IS NOT TO BE HURRIED.
THE SIEGE PERILOUS WILL OPEN THE DOOR, BUT ONLY THE SPELL CAN SUMMON OUR FRIEND.
THERE! IT WORKS!
D-DID HE SAY THE SIEGE PERILOUS? THAT'S THE DEVICE THAT THE GOBLIN USED TO OPEN PORTALS TO OTHER DIMENSIONS!
WHAT ARE THEY UP TO?
OH NO, IT'S THE GOBLIN! NOT MY GOBLIN, BUT...
...THE GOBLIN FROM ANOTHER DIMENSION!

YOU! YOU BROUGHT ME HERE FROM MY WORLD. WHY?
BY THE EYE OF AGAMOTTO! YOU WERE RIGHT, OCTAVIUS! THIS GOBLIN IS TRULY A SIGHT TO BEHOLD!
WELL?!
OF ALL OF THE GOBLINS IN ALL OF THE DIMENSIONS, YOU ARE THE ONLY ONE TO DEFEAT A SPIDER-MAN. HYDRA BROUGHT YOU HERE TO OBLITERATE ANOTHER ONE.
DO YOU BAD GUYS ALWAYS TALK ABOUT ME BEHIND MY BACK?
WHUDD!
EEP!
YOU WERE RIGHT TO BRING ME HERE TO CRUSH SPIDERS--
--IT IS MY FAVORITE PASTIME!
AAAH!
MAN, HATERS GONNA HATE!
WHERE'S A WALL TO WEB TO WHEN YOU NEED ONE?

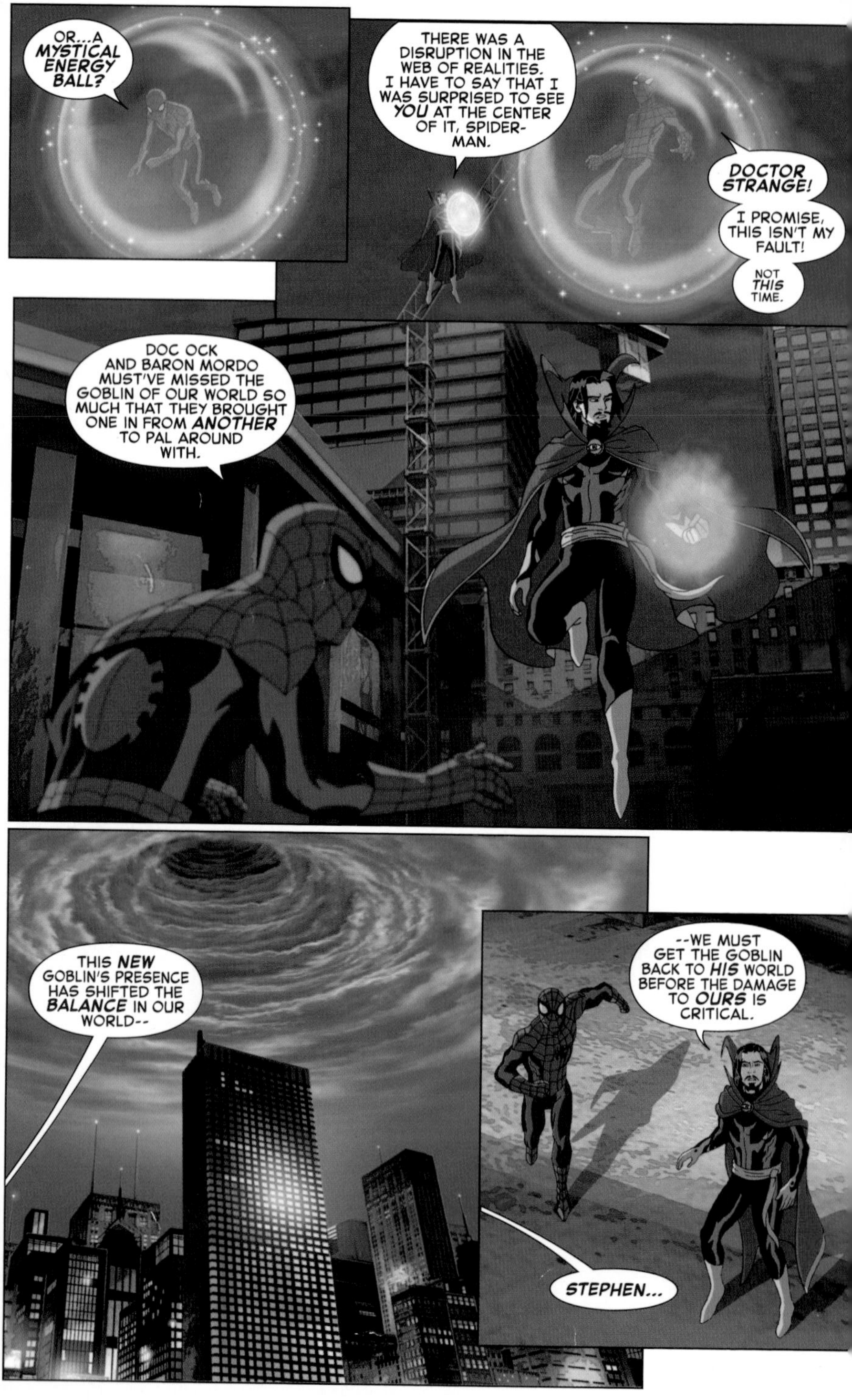
OR...A MYSTICAL ENERGY BALL?
THERE WAS A DISRUPTION IN THE WEB OF REALITIES. I HAVE TO SAY THAT I WAS SURPRISED TO SEE YOU AT THE CENTER OF IT, SPIDER-MAN.
DOCTOR STRANGE!
I PROMISE, THIS ISN'T MY FAULT!
NOT THIS TIME.
DOC OCK AND BARON MORDO MUST'VE MISSED THE GOBLIN OF OUR WORLD SO MUCH THAT THEY BROUGHT ONE IN FROM ANOTHER TO PAL AROUND WITH.
THIS NEW GOBLIN'S PRESENCE HAS SHIFTED THE BALANCE IN OUR WORLD--
--WE MUST GET THE GOBLIN BACK TO HIS WORLD BEFORE THE DAMAGE TO OURS IS CRITICAL.
STEPHEN...

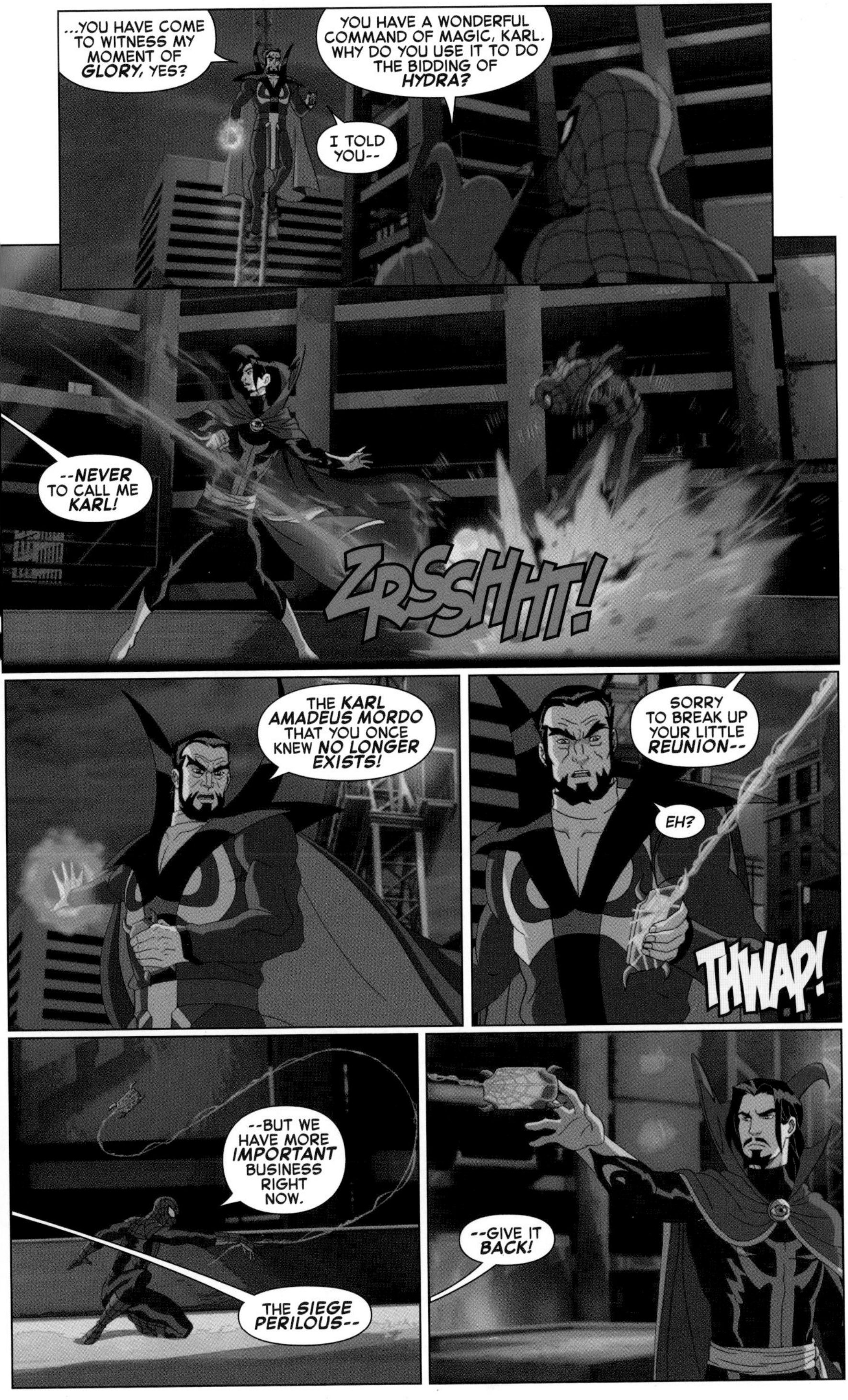
...YOU HAVE COME TO WITNESS MY MOMENT OF GLORY, YES?
YOU HAVE A WONDERFUL COMMAND OF MAGIC, KARL. WHY DO YOU USE IT TO DO THE BIDDING OF HYDRA?
I TOLD YOU--
--NEVER TO CALL ME KARL!
ZRSSHHT!
THE KARL AMADEUS MORDO THAT YOU ONCE KNEW NO LONGER EXISTS!
SORRY TO BREAK UP YOUR LITTLE REUNION--
EH?
THWAP!
--BUT WE HAVE MORE IMPORTANT BUSINESS RIGHT NOW.
THE SIEGE PERILOUS--
--GIVE IT BACK!

THWAP!
HNN!
IS IT REQUIRED FOR SUPER VILLAINS TO TALK WAY TOO MUCH?
THWIP!
THWIP!
STEPHEN STRANGE CANNOT BE TRUSTED WITH THE SIEGE PERILOUS!
THWAP!
AND YOU'RE TRUSTWORTHY? YOU CAN'T EVEN BE TRUSTED WITH YOUR BEARD TRIMMER!
I CAN ONLY KEEP THE PORTAL OPEN FOR A SHORT WHILE!
TRY TO LURE THE GOBLIN BACK HOME THROUGH IT.
DO YOU THINK ME SO FOOLISH THAT I WOULD FALL FOR YOUR TRICKERY?
YIKES!

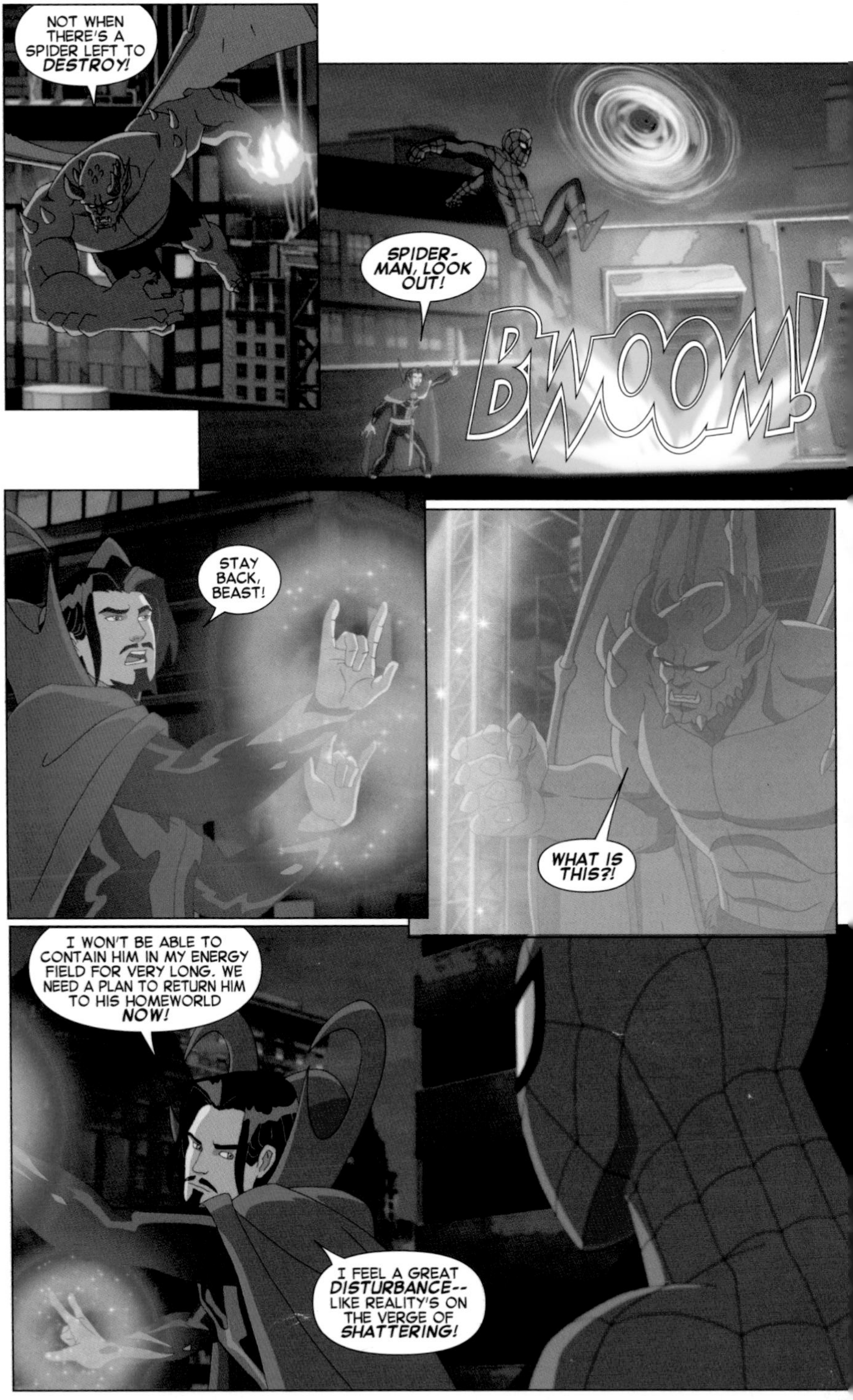
NOT WHEN THERE'S A SPIDER LEFT TO DESTROY!
SPIDER-MAN, LOOK OUT!
BWOOM!
STAY BACK, BEAST!
WHAT IS THIS?!
I WON'T BE ABLE TO CONTAIN HIM IN MY ENERGY FIELD FOR VERY LONG. WE NEED A PLAN TO RETURN HIM TO HIS HOMEWORLD NOW!
I FEEL A GREAT DISTURBANCE-- LIKE REALITY'S ON THE VERGE OF SHATTERING!

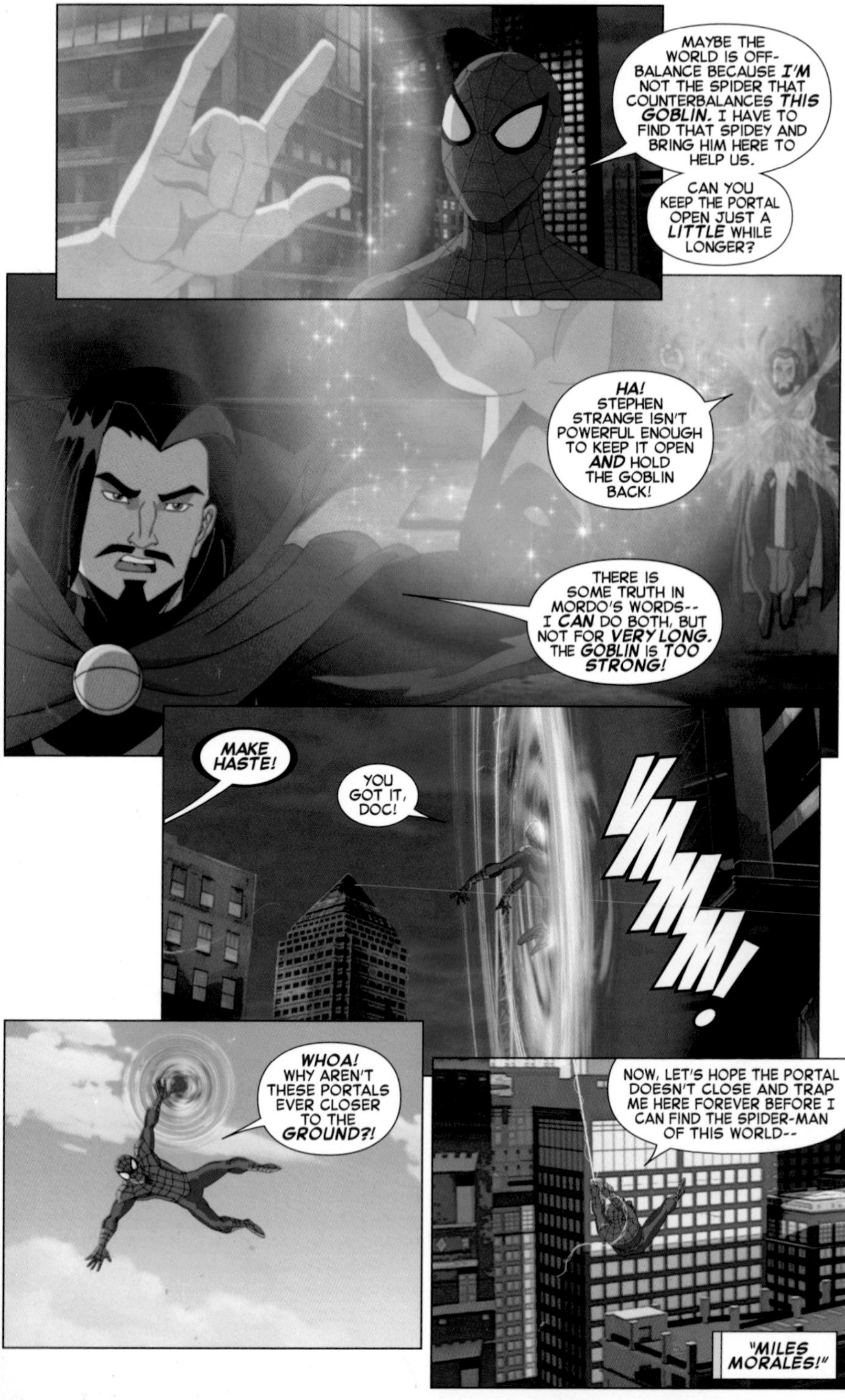
MAYBE THE WORLD IS OFF-BALANCE BECAUSE I'M NOT THE SPIDER THAT COUNTERBALANCES THIS GOBLIN. I HAVE TO FIND THAT SPIDEY AND BRING HIM HERE TO HELP US.
CAN YOU KEEP THE PORTAL OPEN JUST A LITTLE WHILE LONGER?
HA! STEPHEN STRANGE ISN'T POWERFUL ENOUGH TO KEEP IT OPEN AND HOLD THE GOBLIN BACK!
THERE IS SOME TRUTH IN MORDO'S WORDS-- I CAN DO BOTH, BUT NOT FOR VERY LONG. THE GOBLIN IS TOO STRONG!
MAKE HASTE!
YOU GOT IT, DOC!
VMMMM!
WHOA! WHY AREN'T THESE PORTALS EVER CLOSER TO THE GROUND?!
NOW, LET'S HOPE THE PORTAL DOESN'T CLOSE AND TRAP ME HERE FOREVER BEFORE I CAN FIND THE SPIDER-MAN OF THIS WORLD--
"MILES MORALES!"

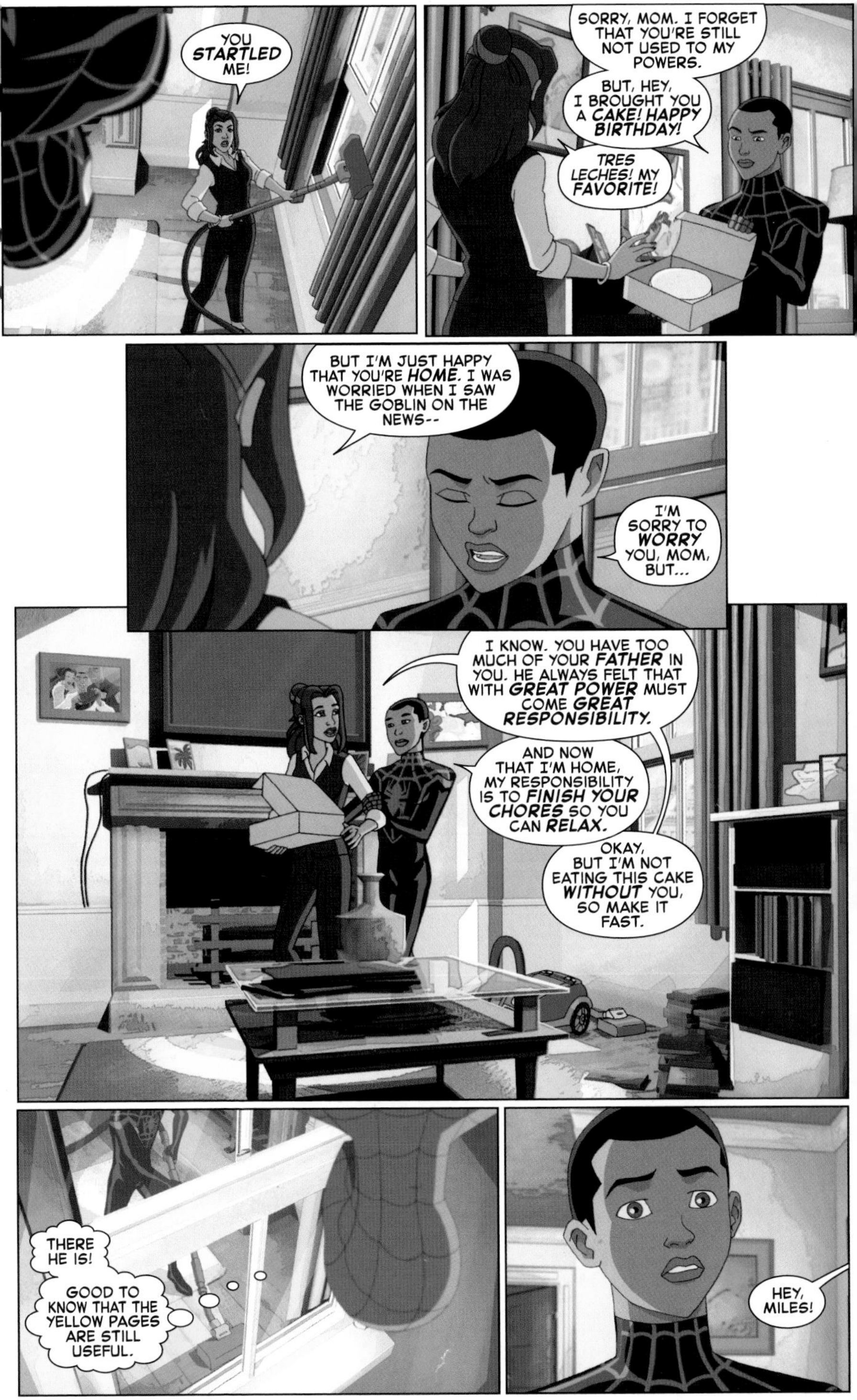
YOU STARTLED ME!
SORRY, MOM. I FORGET THAT YOU'RE STILL NOT USED TO MY POWERS.
BUT, HEY, I BROUGHT YOU A CAKE! HAPPY BIRTHDAY!
TRES LECHES! MY FAVORITE!
BUT I'M JUST HAPPY THAT YOU'RE HOME. I WAS WORRIED WHEN I SAW THE GOBLIN ON THE NEWS--
I'M SORRY TO WORRY YOU, MOM, BUT...
I KNOW. YOU HAVE TOO MUCH OF YOUR FATHER IN YOU. HE ALWAYS FELT THAT WITH GREAT POWER MUST COME GREAT RESPONSIBILITY.
AND NOW THAT I'M HOME, MY RESPONSIBILITY IS TO FINISH YOUR CHORES SO YOU CAN RELAX.
OKAY, BUT I'M NOT EATING THIS CAKE WITHOUT YOU, SO MAKE IT FAST.
THERE HE IS!
GOOD TO KNOW THAT THE YELLOW PAGES ARE STILL USEFUL.
HEY, MILES!

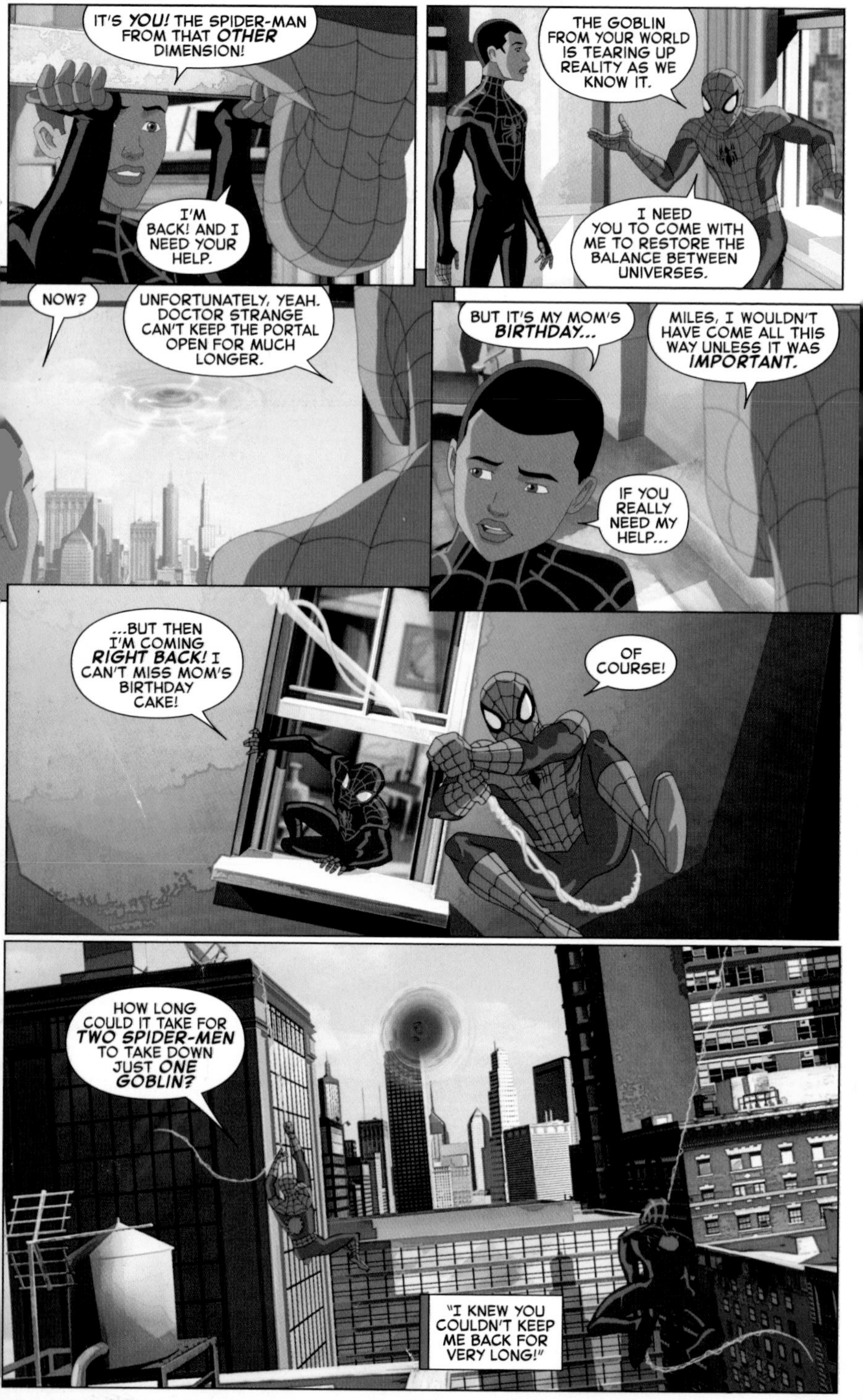
IT'S YOU! THE SPIDER-MAN FROM THAT OTHER DIMENSION!
I'M BACK! AND I NEED YOUR HELP.
THE GOBLIN FROM YOUR WORLD IS TEARING UP REALITY AS WE KNOW IT.
I NEED YOU TO COME WITH ME TO RESTORE THE BALANCE BETWEEN UNIVERSES.
NOW?
UNFORTUNATELY, YEAH. DOCTOR STRANGE CAN'T KEEP THE PORTAL OPEN FOR MUCH LONGER.
BUT IT'S MY MOM'S BIRTHDAY...
MILES, I WOULDN'T HAVE COME ALL THIS WAY UNLESS IT WAS IMPORTANT.
IF YOU REALLY NEED MY HELP...
...BUT THEN I'M COMING RIGHT BACK! I CAN'T MISS MOM'S BIRTHDAY CAKE!
OF COURSE!
HOW LONG COULD IT TAKE FOR TWO SPIDER-MEN TO TAKE DOWN JUST ONE GOBLIN?
"I KNEW YOU COULDN'T KEEP ME BACK FOR VERY LONG!"

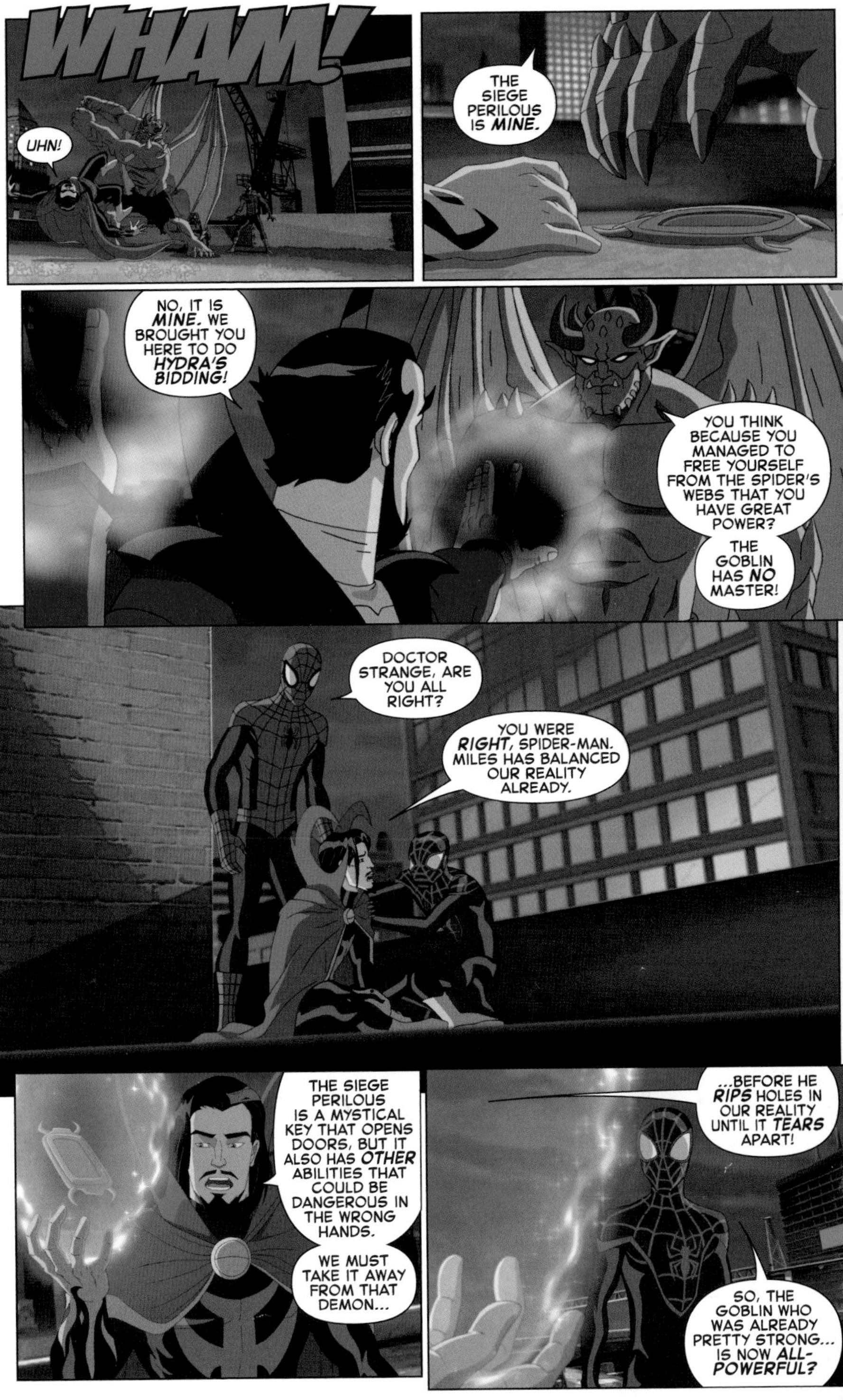
WHAM!
UHN!
THE SIEGE PERILOUS IS MINE.
NO, IT IS MINE. WE BROUGHT YOU HERE TO DO HYDRA'S BIDDING!
YOU THINK BECAUSE YOU MANAGED TO FREE YOURSELF FROM THE SPIDER'S WEBS THAT YOU HAVE GREAT POWER?
THE GOBLIN HAS NO MASTER!
DOCTOR STRANGE, ARE YOU ALL RIGHT?
YOU WERE RIGHT, SPIDER-MAN. MILES HAS BALANCED OUR REALITY ALREADY.
THE SIEGE PERILOUS IS A MYSTICAL KEY THAT OPENS DOORS, BUT IT ALSO HAS OTHER ABILITIES THAT COULD BE DANGEROUS IN THE WRONG HANDS.
WE MUST TAKE IT AWAY FROM THAT DEMON...
...BEFORE HE RIPS HOLES IN OUR REALITY UNTIL IT TEARS APART!
SO, THE GOBLIN WHO WAS ALREADY PRETTY STRONG... IS NOW ALL-POWERFUL?

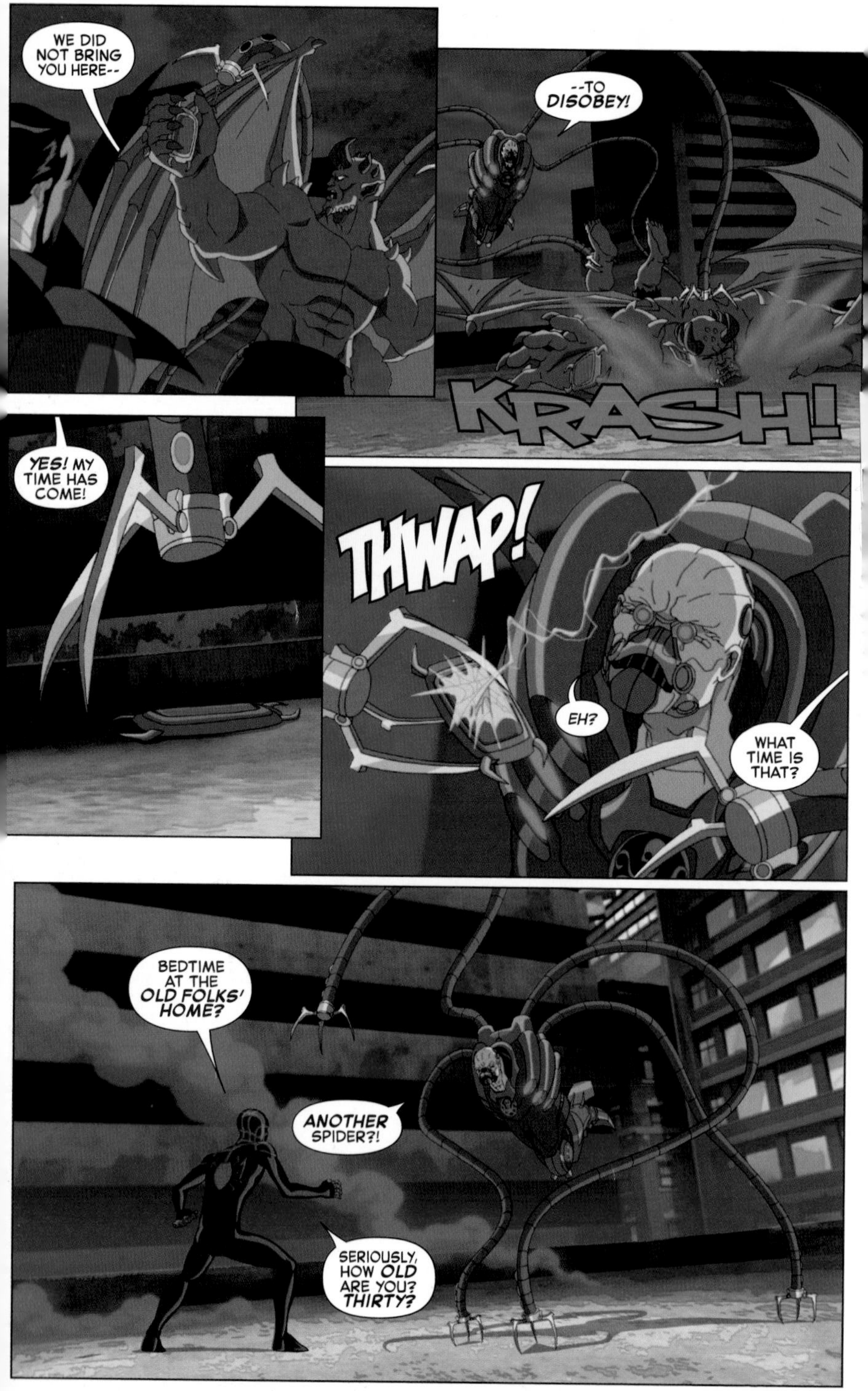
WE DID NOT BRING YOU HERE--
--TO DISOBEY!
KRASH!
YES! MY TIME HAS COME!
THWAP!
EH?
WHAT TIME IS THAT?
BEDTIME AT THE OLD FOLKS' HOME?
ANOTHER SPIDER?!
SERIOUSLY, HOW OLD ARE YOU? THIRTY?

AND YOU ARE JUST AS OBNOXIOUS AS THE *OTHER* SPIDER!
ZRSSH!
NNNNN...
FOOL.
KROOM!
DO YOU BELIEVE ANYONE IS MORE WORTHY THAN *I* TO CONTROL THE *SIEGE PERILOUS?*

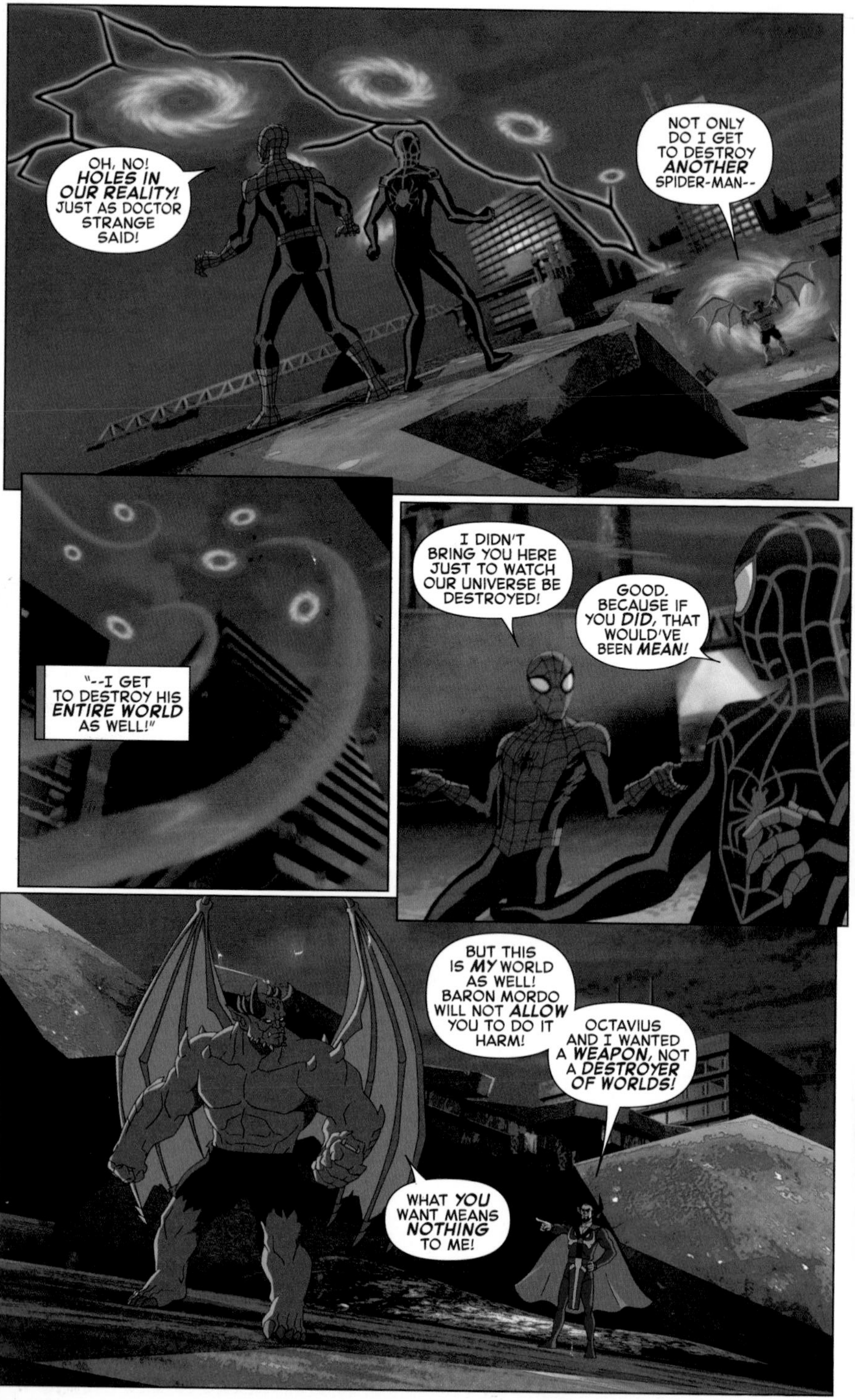
OH, NO! HOLES IN OUR REALITY! JUST AS DOCTOR STRANGE SAID!
NOT ONLY DO I GET TO DESTROY ANOTHER SPIDER-MAN--
"--I GET TO DESTROY HIS ENTIRE WORLD AS WELL!"
I DIDN'T BRING YOU HERE JUST TO WATCH OUR UNIVERSE BE DESTROYED!
GOOD. BECAUSE IF YOU DID, THAT WOULD'VE BEEN MEAN!
BUT THIS IS MY WORLD AS WELL! BARON MORDO WILL NOT ALLOW YOU TO DO IT HARM!
OCTAVIUS AND I WANTED A WEAPON, NOT A DESTROYER OF WORLDS!
WHAT YOU WANT MEANS NOTHING TO ME!

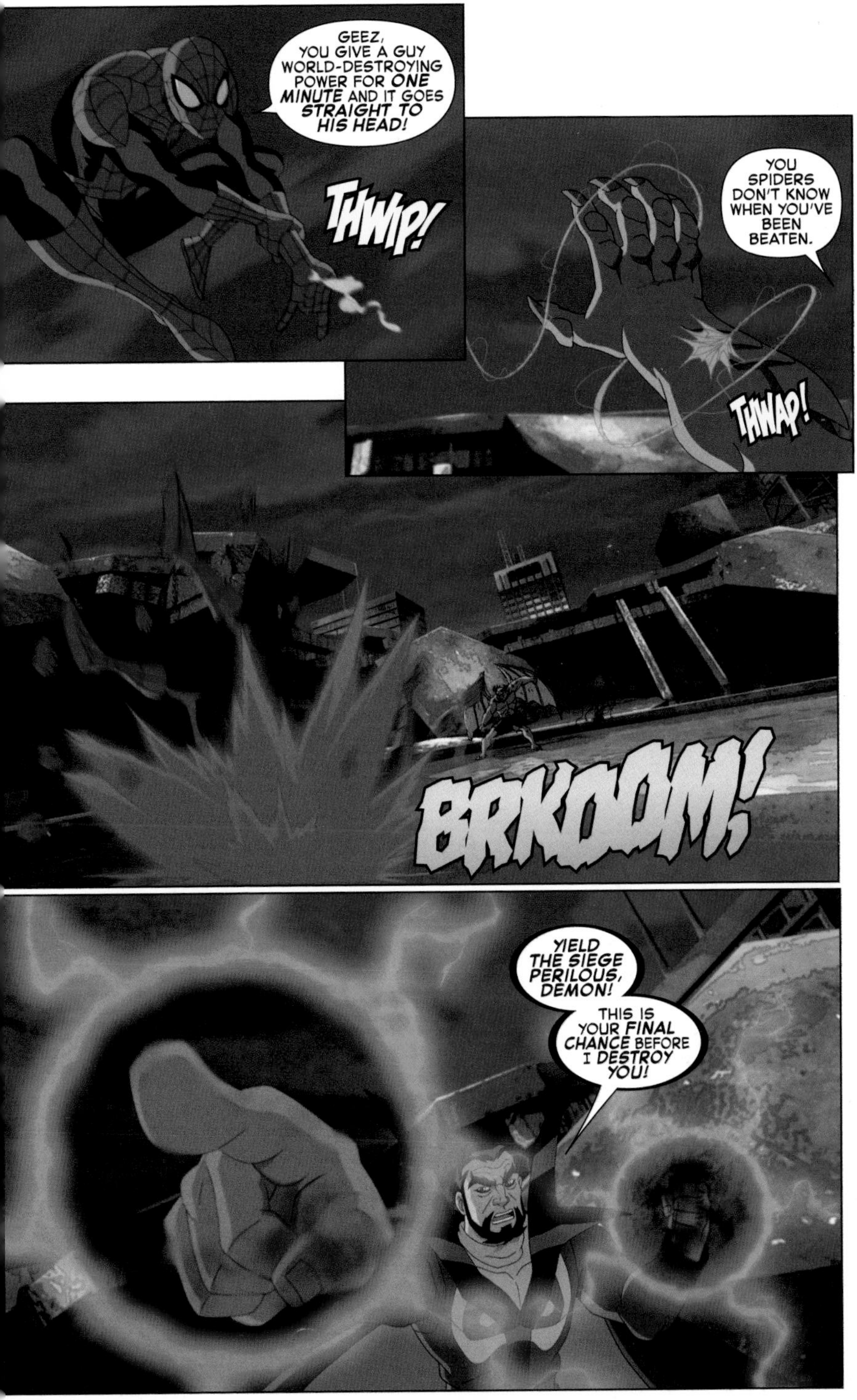
GEEZ, YOU GIVE A GUY WORLD-DESTROYING POWER FOR ONE MINUTE AND IT GOES STRAIGHT TO HIS HEAD!
THWIP!
YOU SPIDERS DON'T KNOW WHEN YOU'VE BEEN BEATEN.
THWAP!
BRKOOM!
YIELD THE SIEGE PERILOUS, DEMON!
THIS IS YOUR FINAL CHANCE BEFORE I DESTROY YOU!

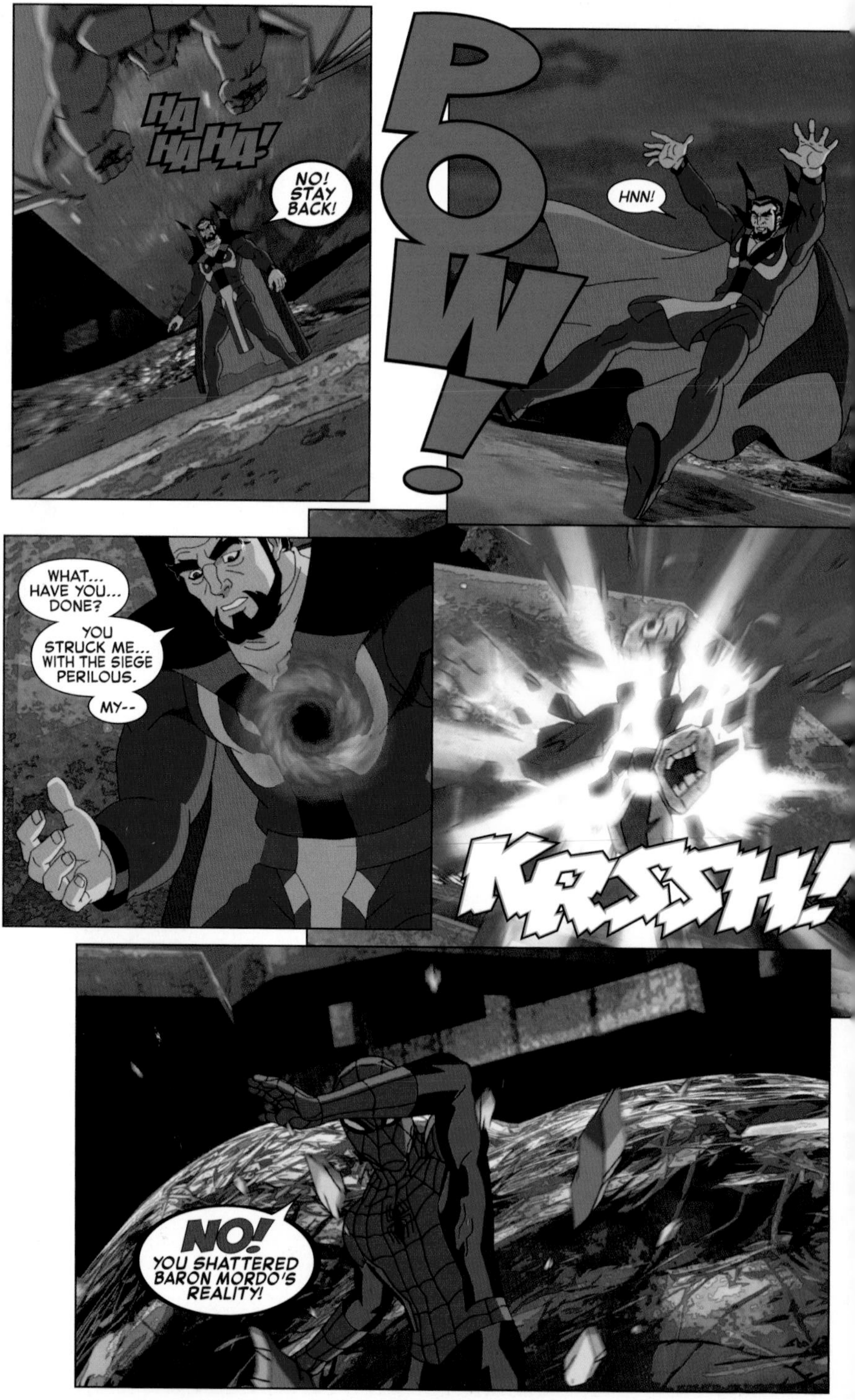
HA HA HA HA!
NO! STAY BACK!
POW!
HNN!
WHAT... HAVE YOU... DONE?
YOU STRUCK ME... WITH THE SIEGE PERILOUS.
MY--
KRSSH!
NO! YOU SHATTERED BARON MORDO'S REALITY!

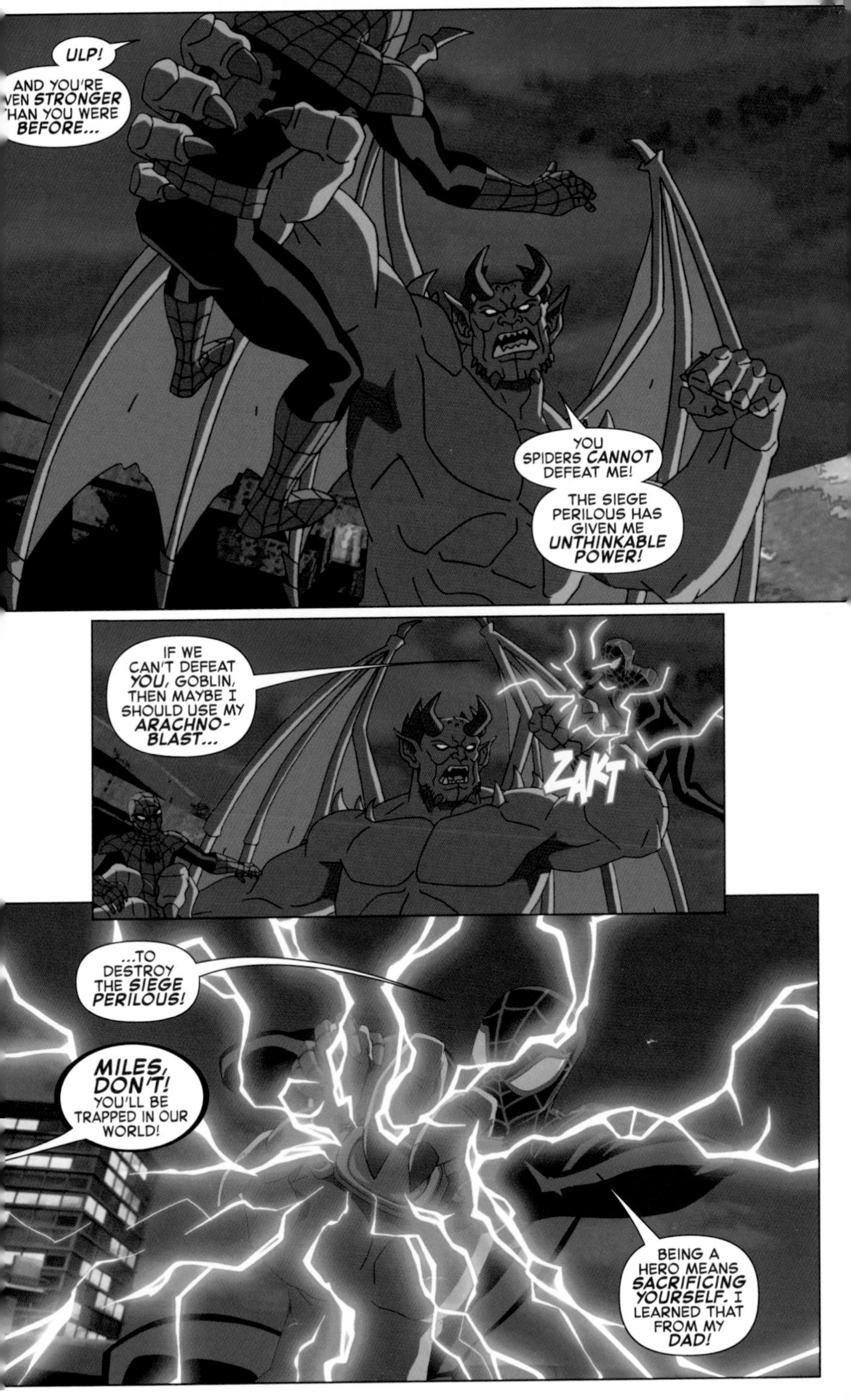
ULP!
AND YOU'RE VEN STRONGER HAN YOU WERE BEFORE...
YOU SPIDERS CANNOT DEFEAT ME!
THE SIEGE PERILOUS HAS GIVEN ME UNTHINKABLE POWER!
IF WE CAN'T DEFEAT YOU, GOBLIN, THEN MAYBE I SHOULD USE MY ARACHNO-BLAST...
ZAKT
...TO DESTROY THE SIEGE PERILOUS!
MILES, DON'T! YOU'LL BE TRAPPED IN OUR WORLD!
BEING A HERO MEANS SACRIFICING YOURSELF. I LEARNED THAT FROM MY DAD!

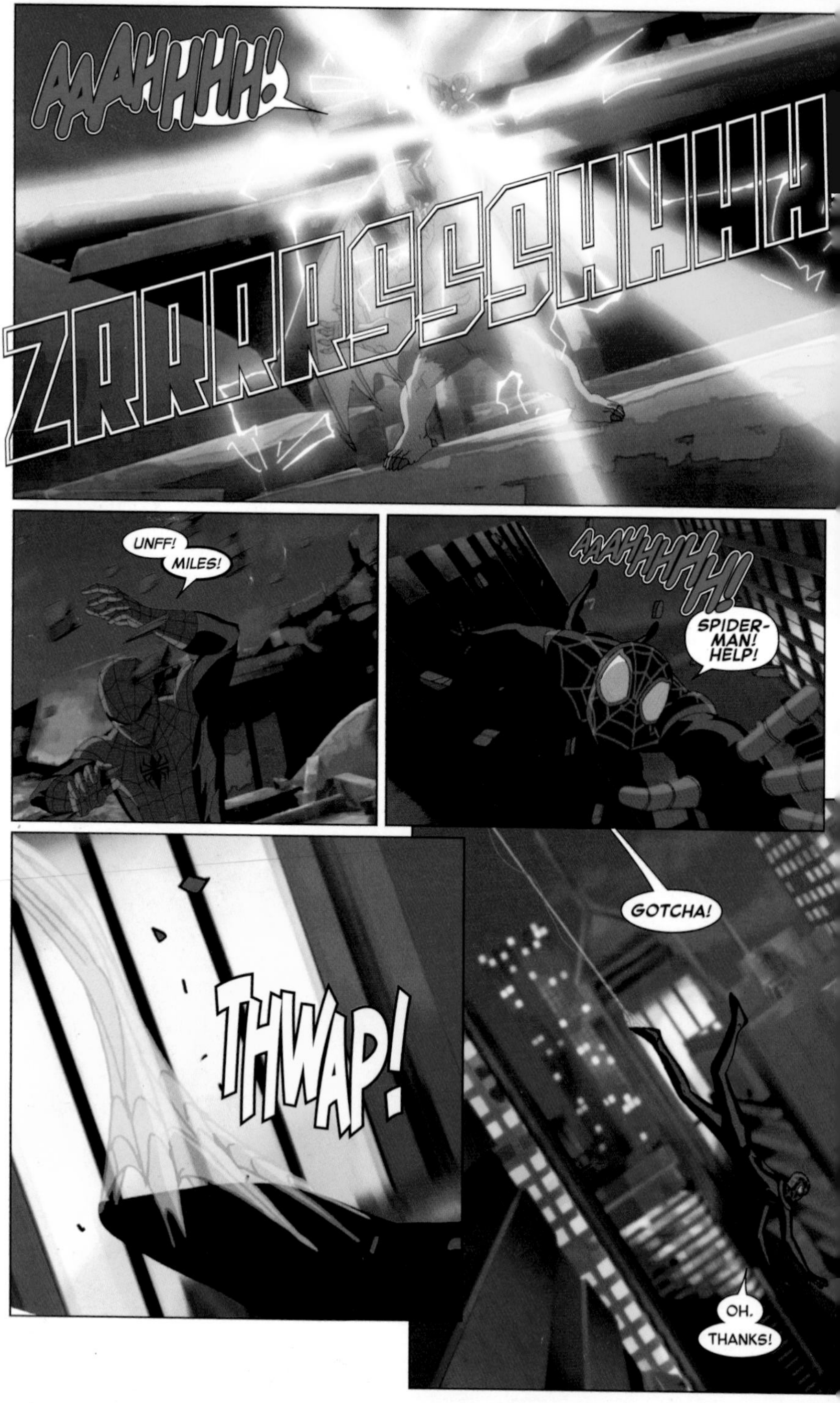
AAAHHHH!
ZRRRSSSHHHH
UNFF! MILES!
AAAHHHHH!
SPIDER-MAN! HELP!
THWAP!
GOTCHA!
OH. THANKS!

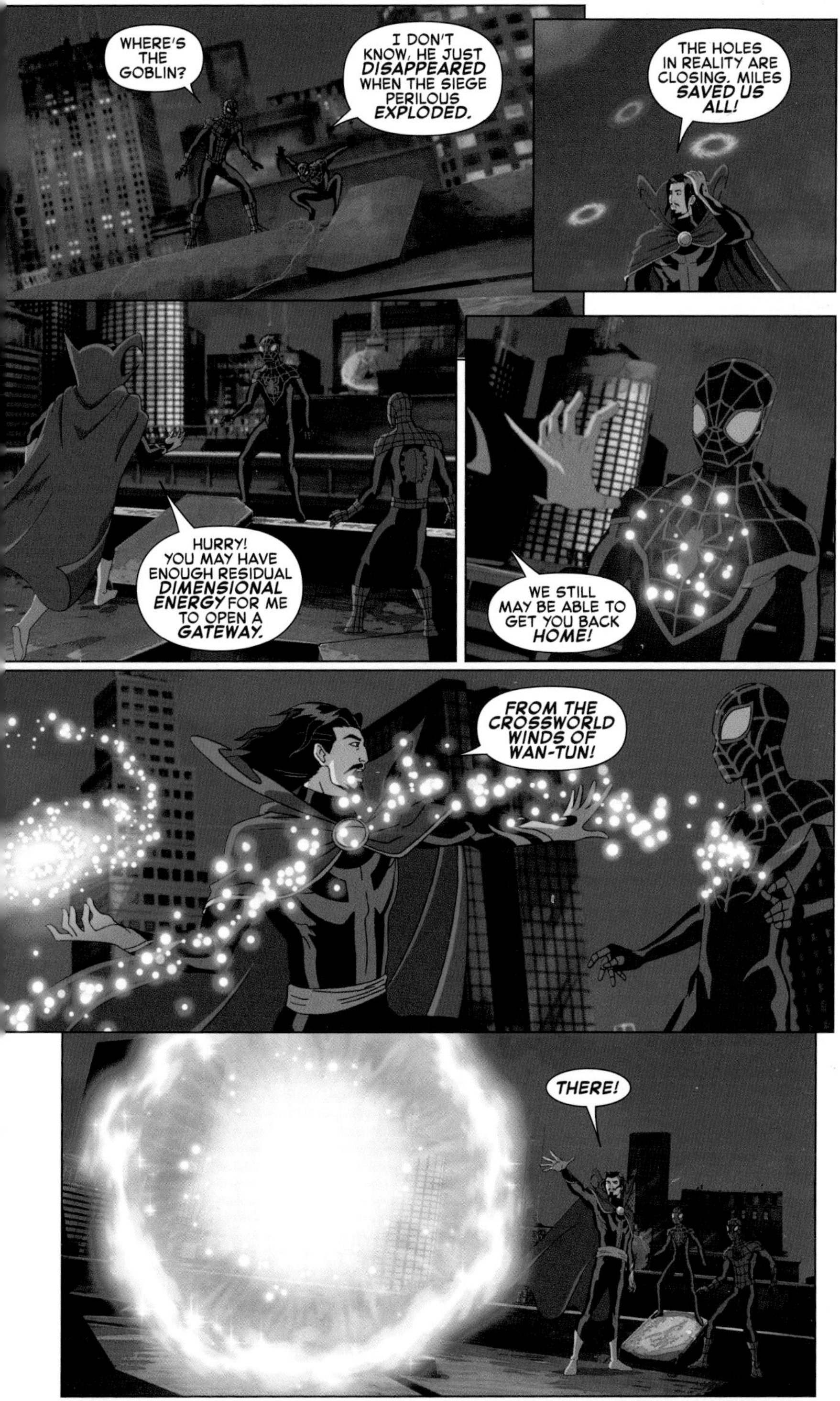
WHERE'S THE GOBLIN?
I DON'T KNOW, HE JUST DISAPPEARED WHEN THE SIEGE PERILOUS EXPLODED.
THE HOLES IN REALITY ARE CLOSING. MILES SAVED US ALL!
HURRY! YOU MAY HAVE ENOUGH RESIDUAL DIMENSIONAL ENERGY FOR ME TO OPEN A GATEWAY.
WE STILL MAY BE ABLE TO GET YOU BACK HOME!
FROM THE CROSSWORLD WINDS OF WAN-TUN!
THERE!

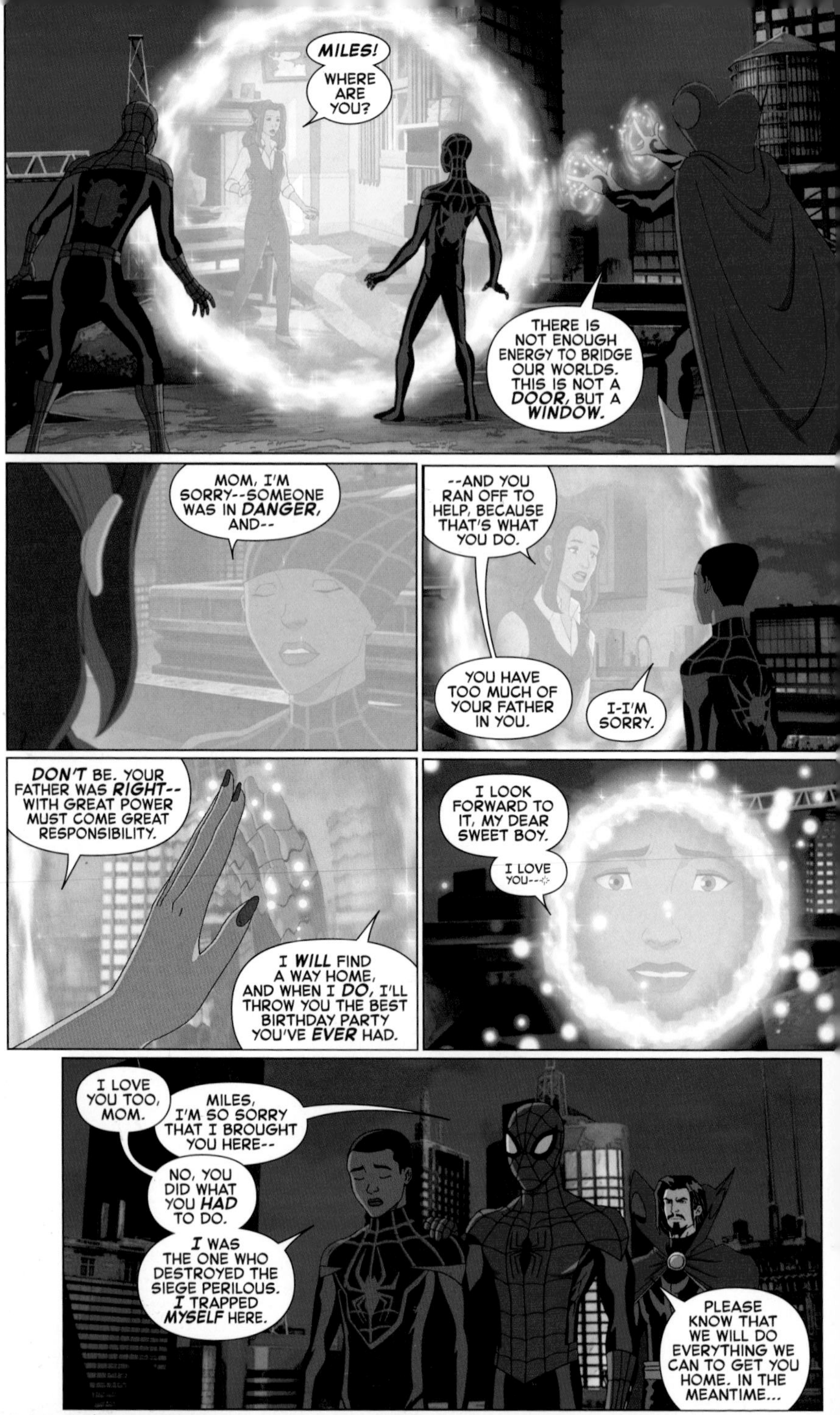
MILES! WHERE ARE YOU?
THERE IS NOT ENOUGH ENERGY TO BRIDGE OUR WORLDS. THIS IS NOT A DOOR, BUT A WINDOW.
MOM, I'M SORRY--SOMEONE WAS IN DANGER, AND--
--AND YOU RAN OFF TO HELP, BECAUSE THAT'S WHAT YOU DO.
YOU HAVE TOO MUCH OF YOUR FATHER IN YOU.
I-I'M SORRY.
DON'T BE. YOUR FATHER WAS RIGHT-- WITH GREAT POWER MUST COME GREAT RESPONSIBILITY.
I WILL FIND A WAY HOME, AND WHEN I DO, I'LL THROW YOU THE BEST BIRTHDAY PARTY YOU'VE EVER HAD.
I LOOK FORWARD TO IT, MY DEAR SWEET BOY.
I LOVE YOU--
I LOVE YOU TOO, MOM.
MILES, I'M SO SORRY THAT I BROUGHT YOU HERE--
NO, YOU DID WHAT YOU HAD TO DO.
I WAS THE ONE WHO DESTROYED THE SIEGE PERILOUS. I TRAPPED MYSELF HERE.
PLEASE KNOW THAT WE WILL DO EVERYTHING WE CAN TO GET YOU HOME. IN THE MEANTIME...

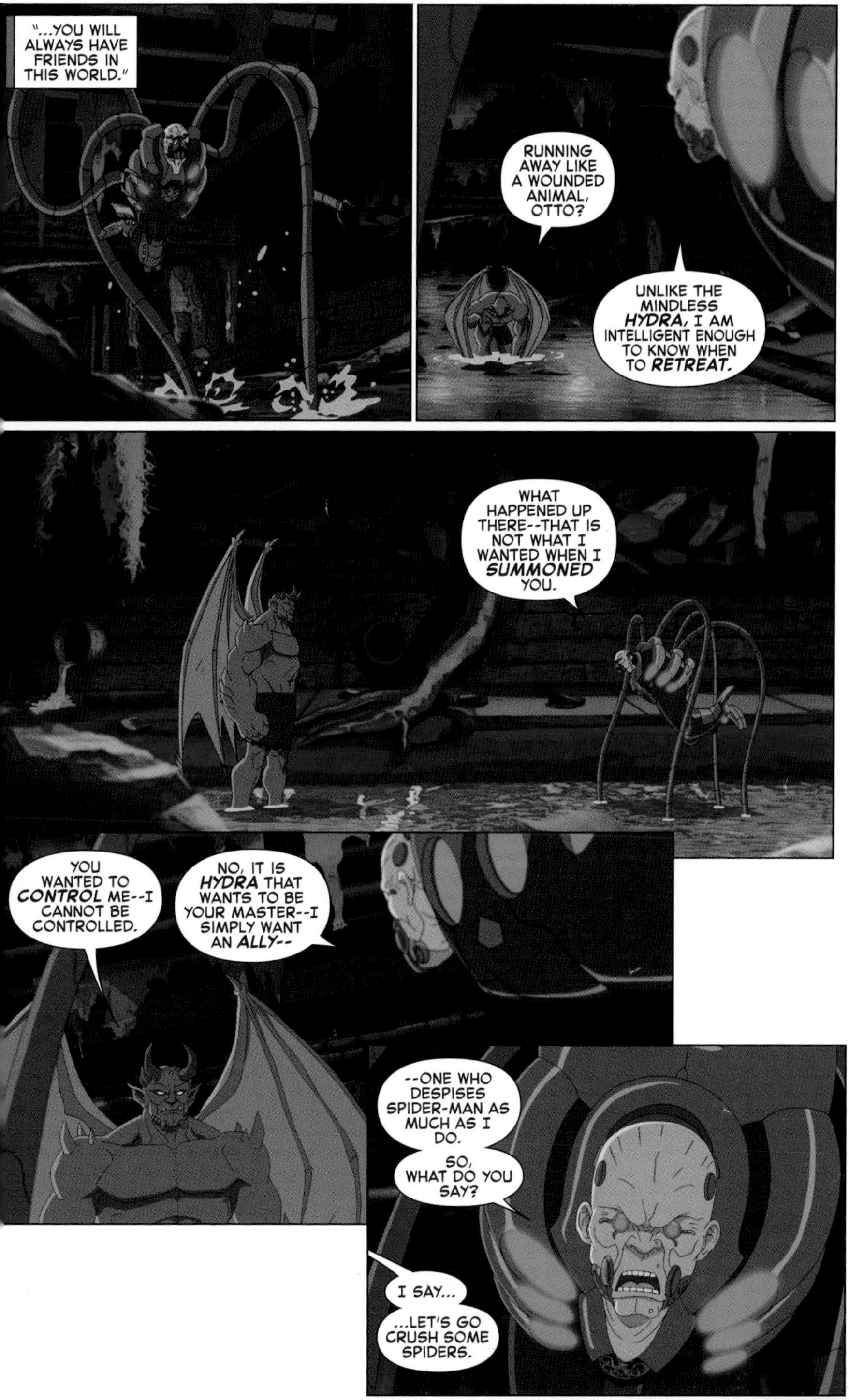
"...YOU WILL ALWAYS HAVE FRIENDS IN THIS WORLD."
RUNNING AWAY LIKE A WOUNDED ANIMAL, OTTO?
UNLIKE THE MINDLESS HYDRA, I AM INTELLIGENT ENOUGH TO KNOW WHEN TO RETREAT.
WHAT HAPPENED UP THERE--THAT IS NOT WHAT I WANTED WHEN I SUMMONED YOU.
YOU WANTED TO CONTROL ME--I CANNOT BE CONTROLLED.
NO, IT IS HYDRA THAT WANTS TO BE YOUR MASTER--I SIMPLY WANT AN ALLY--
--ONE WHO DESPISES SPIDER-MAN AS MUCH AS I DO.
SO, WHAT DO YOU SAY?
I SAY...
...LET'S GO CRUSH SOME SPIDERS.

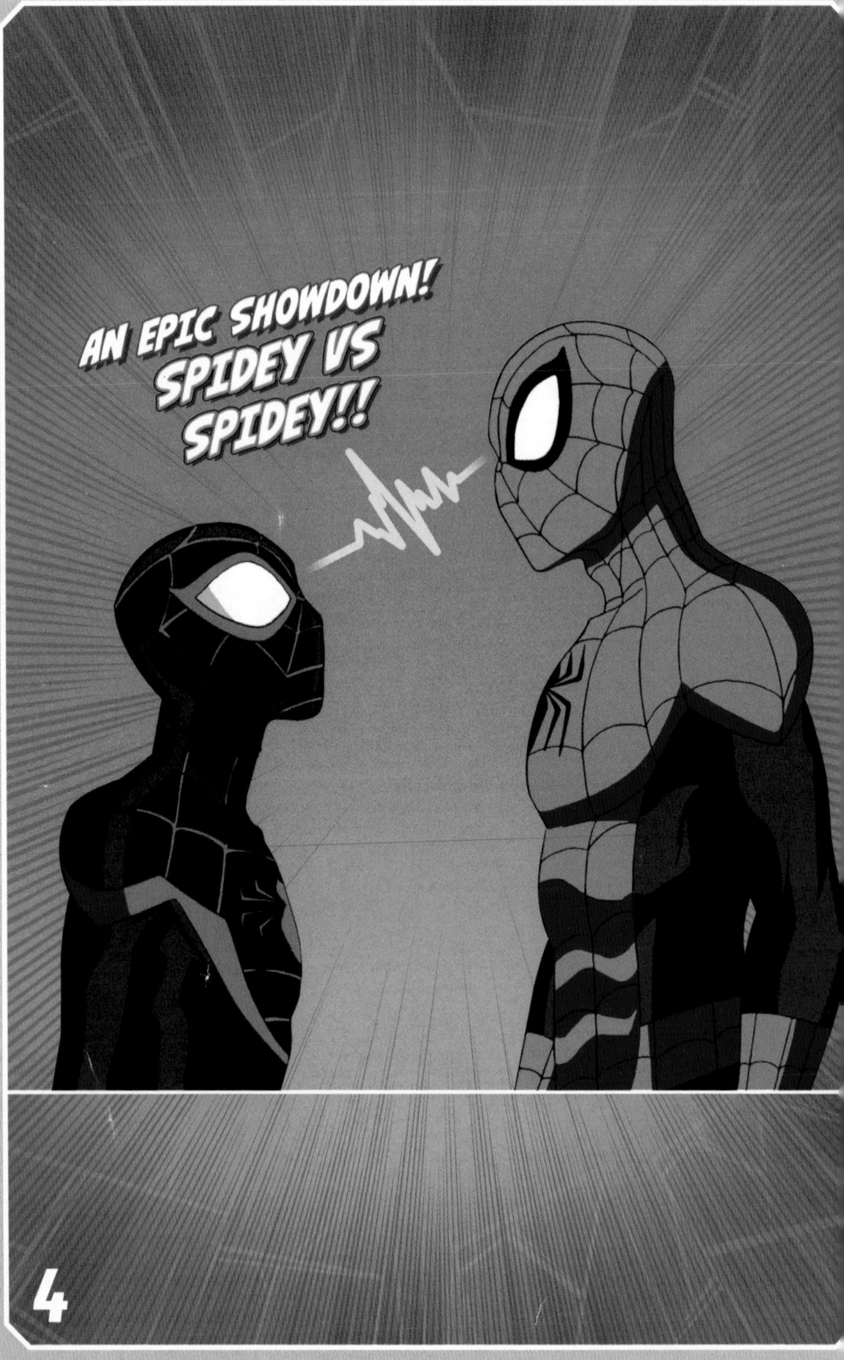
AN EPIC SHOWDOWN! SPIDEY VS SPIDEY!!

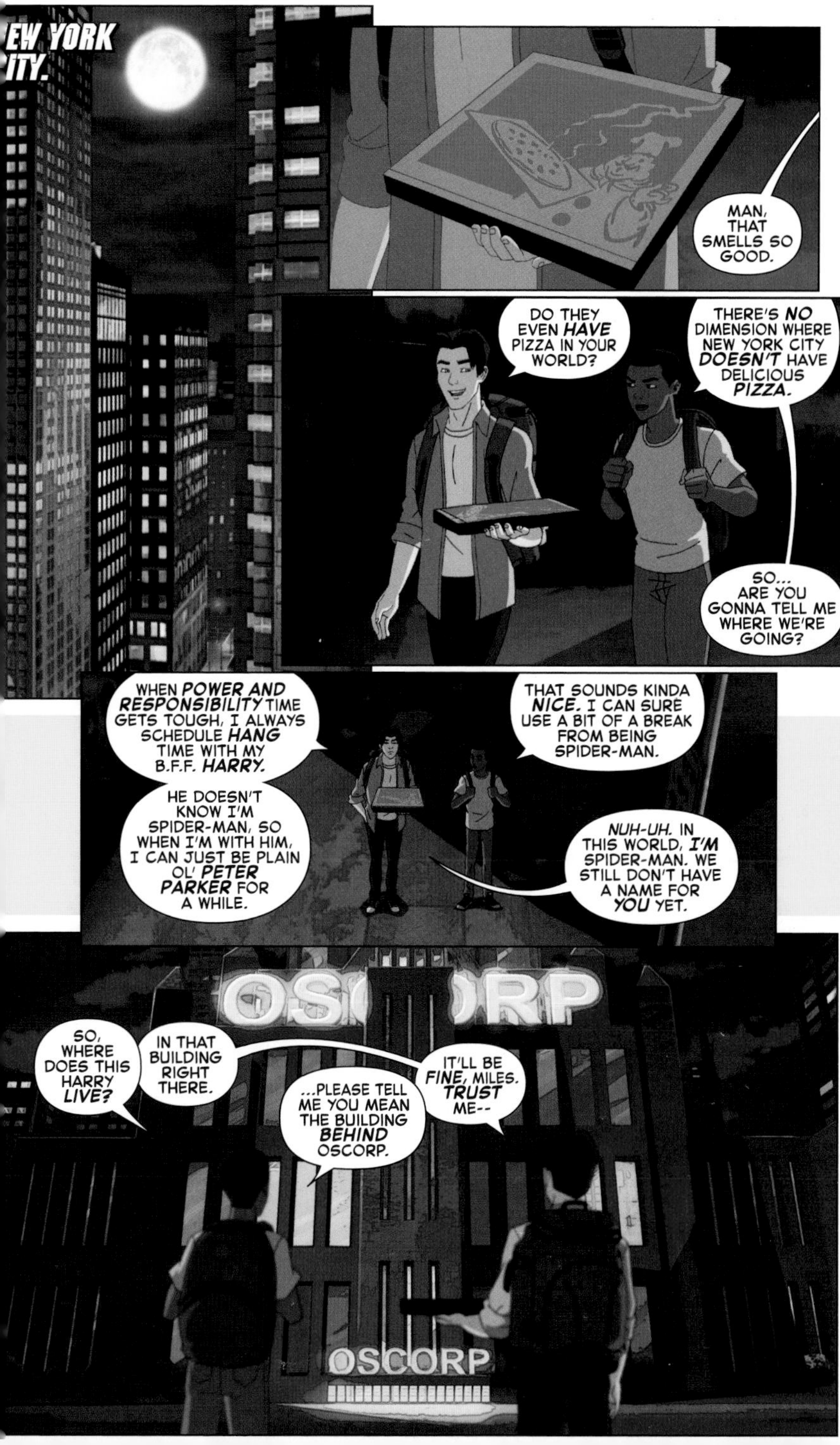
EW YORK
ITY.
MAN, THAT SMELLS SO GOOD.
DO THEY EVEN HAVE PIZZA IN YOUR WORLD?
THERE'S NO DIMENSION WHERE NEW YORK CITY DOESN'T HAVE DELICIOUS PIZZA.
SO... ARE YOU GONNA TELL ME WHERE WE'RE GOING?
WHEN POWER AND RESPONSIBILITY TIME GETS TOUGH, I ALWAYS SCHEDULE HANG TIME WITH MY B.F.F. HARRY.
HE DOESN'T KNOW I'M SPIDER-MAN, SO WHEN I'M WITH HIM, I CAN JUST BE PLAIN OL' PETER PARKER FOR A WHILE.
THAT SOUNDS KINDA NICE. I CAN SURE USE A BIT OF A BREAK FROM BEING SPIDER-MAN.
NUH-UH. IN THIS WORLD, I'M SPIDER-MAN. WE STILL DON'T HAVE A NAME FOR YOU YET.
OSCORP
SO, WHERE DOES THIS HARRY LIVE?
IN THAT BUILDING RIGHT THERE.
...PLEASE TELL ME YOU MEAN THE BUILDING BEHIND OSCORP.
IT'LL BE FINE, MILES. TRUST ME--
OSCORP

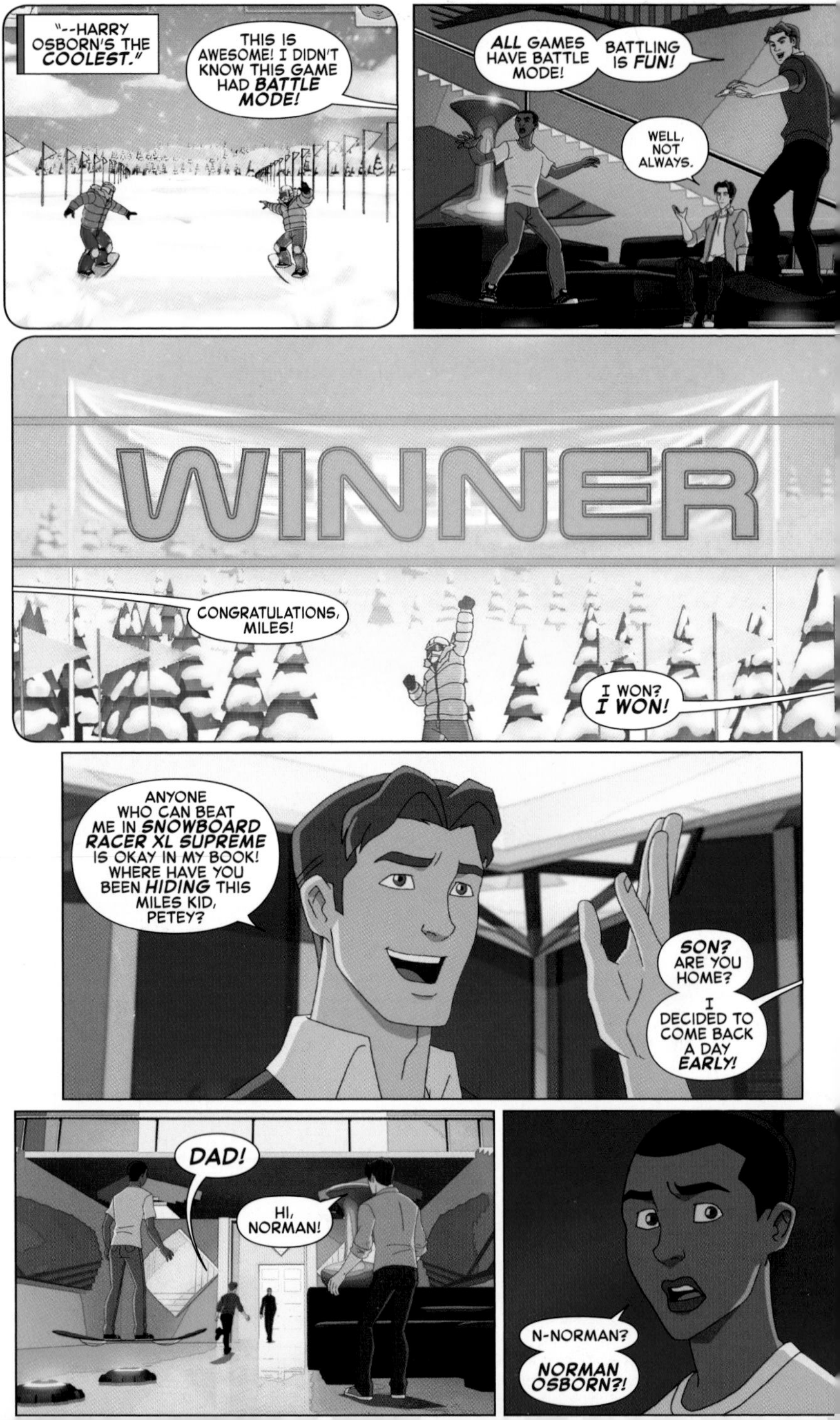

"--HARRY OSBORN'S THE COOLEST."
THIS IS AWESOME! I DIDN'T KNOW THIS GAME HAD BATTLE MODE!
ALL GAMES HAVE BATTLE MODE!
BATTLING IS FUN!
WELL, NOT ALWAYS.
WINNER
CONGRATULATIONS, MILES!
I WON? I WON!
ANYONE WHO CAN BEAT ME IN SNOWBOARD RACER XL SUPREME IS OKAY IN MY BOOK! WHERE HAVE YOU BEEN HIDING THIS MILES KID, PETEY?
SON? ARE YOU HOME?
I DECIDED TO COME BACK A DAY EARLY!
DAD!
HI, NORMAN!
N-NORMAN?
NORMAN OSBORN?!

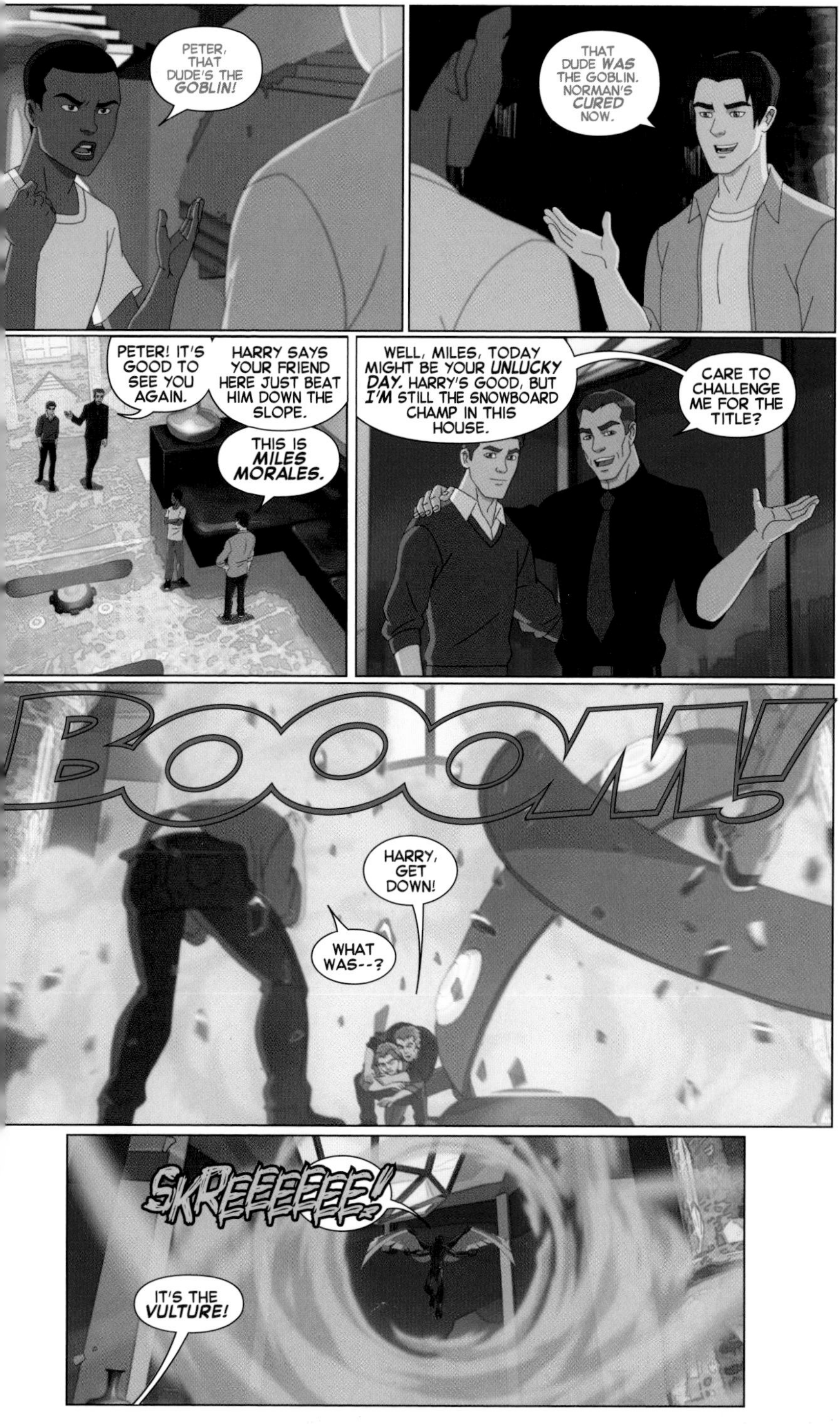
PETER, THAT DUDE'S THE GOBLIN!
THAT DUDE WAS THE GOBLIN. NORMAN'S CURED NOW.
PETER! IT'S GOOD TO SEE YOU AGAIN.
HARRY SAYS YOUR FRIEND HERE JUST BEAT HIM DOWN THE SLOPE.
THIS IS MILES MORALES.
WELL, MILES, TODAY MIGHT BE YOUR UNLUCKY DAY. HARRY'S GOOD, BUT I'M STILL THE SNOWBOARD CHAMP IN THIS HOUSE.
CARE TO CHALLENGE ME FOR THE TITLE?
BOOOM!
HARRY, GET DOWN!
WHAT WAS--?
SKREEEEEEE!
IT'S THE VULTURE!

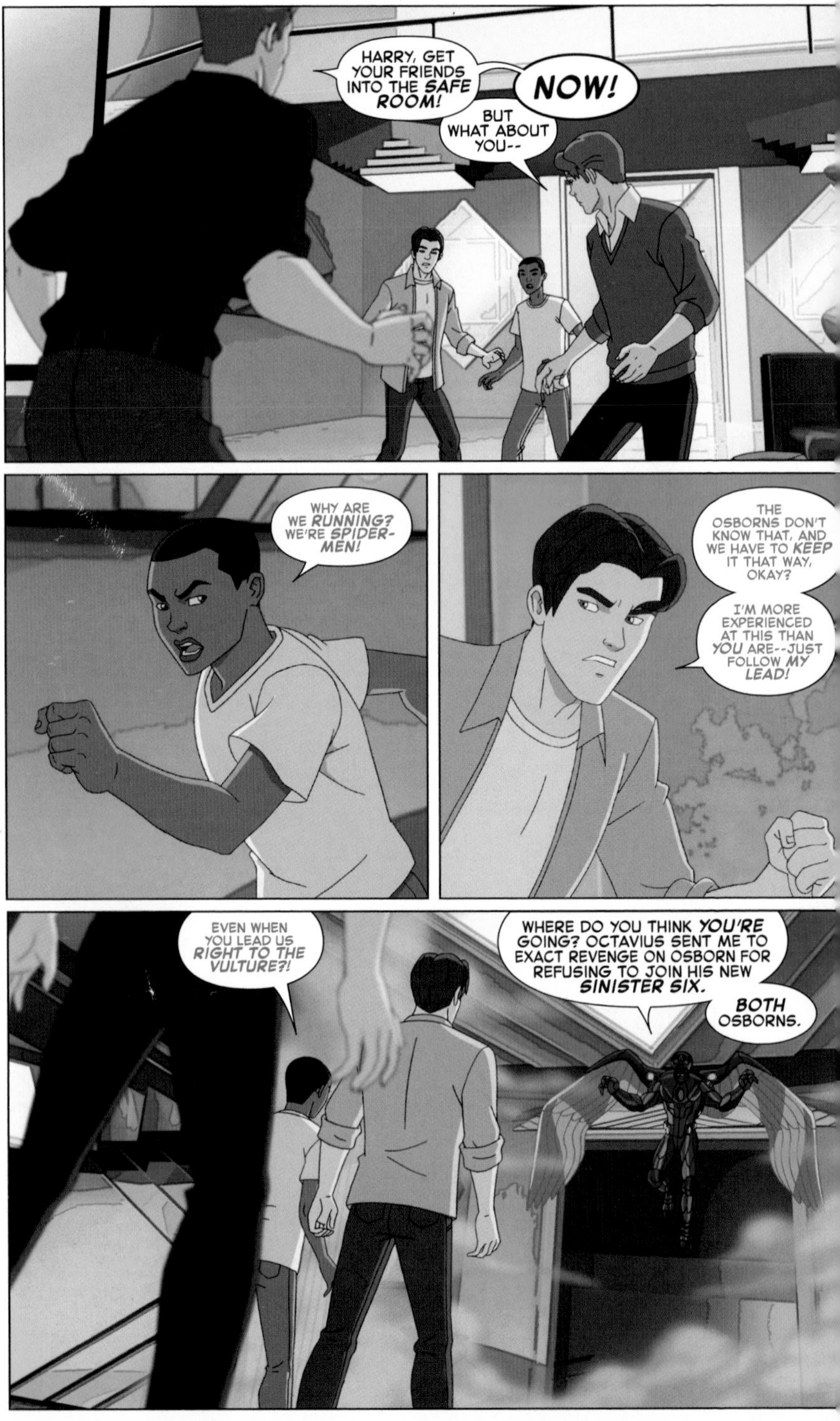
HARRY, GET YOUR FRIENDS INTO THE SAFE ROOM!
NOW!
BUT WHAT ABOUT YOU--
WHY ARE WE RUNNING? WE'RE SPIDER-MEN!
THE OSBORNS DON'T KNOW THAT, AND WE HAVE TO KEEP IT THAT WAY, OKAY?
I'M MORE EXPERIENCED AT THIS THAN YOU ARE--JUST FOLLOW MY LEAD!
EVEN WHEN YOU LEAD US RIGHT TO THE VULTURE?!
WHERE DO YOU THINK YOU'RE GOING? OCTAVIUS SENT ME TO EXACT REVENGE ON OSBORN FOR REFUSING TO JOIN HIS NEW SINISTER SIX.
BOTH OSBORNS.

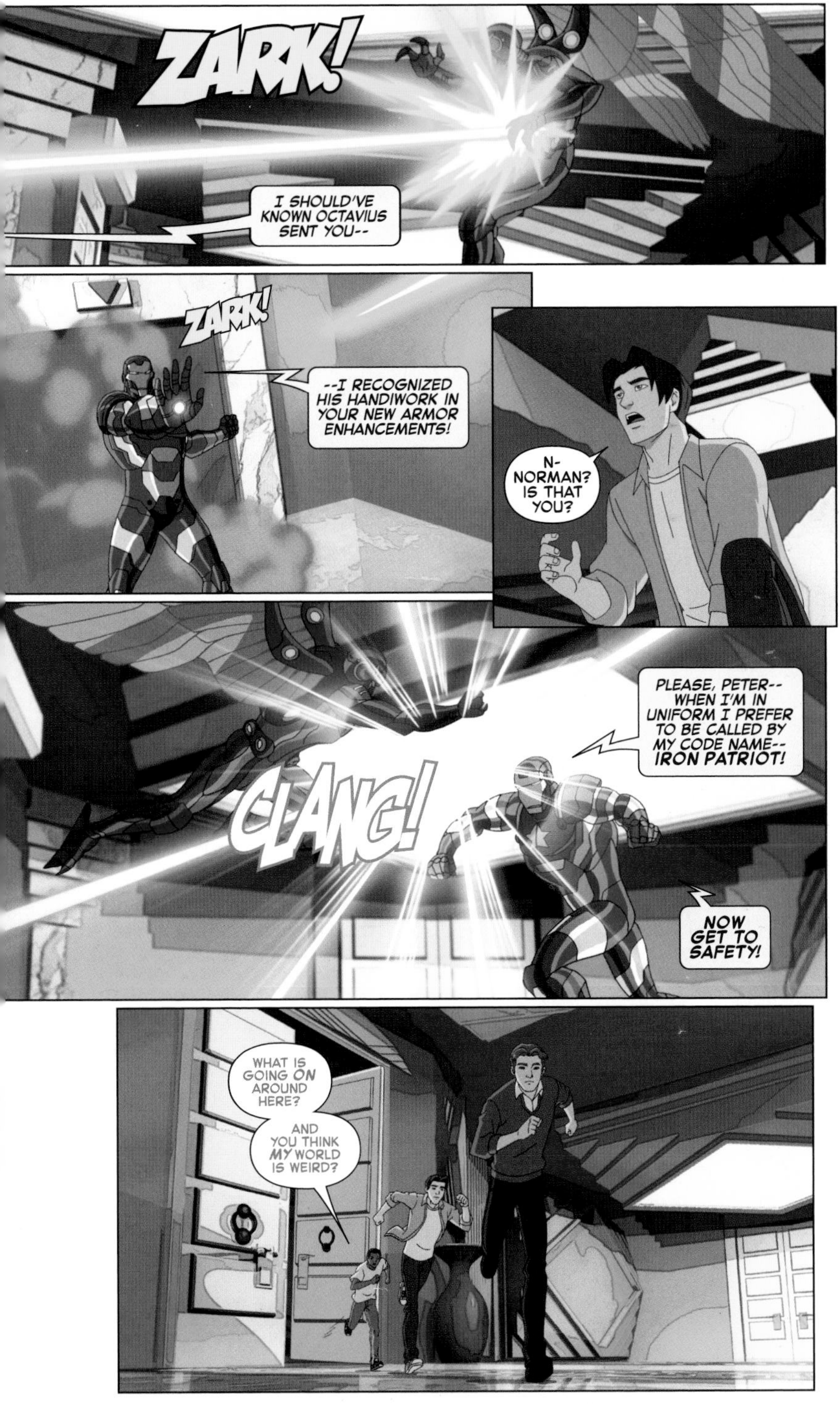
ZARK!
I SHOULD'VE KNOWN OCTAVIUS SENT YOU--
ZARK!
--I RECOGNIZED HIS HANDIWORK IN YOUR NEW ARMOR ENHANCEMENTS!
N- NORMAN? IS THAT YOU?
PLEASE, PETER-- WHEN I'M IN UNIFORM I PREFER TO BE CALLED BY MY CODE NAME-- IRON PATRIOT!
CLANG!
NOW GET TO SAFETY!
WHAT IS GOING ON AROUND HERE?
AND YOU THINK MY WORLD IS WEIRD?

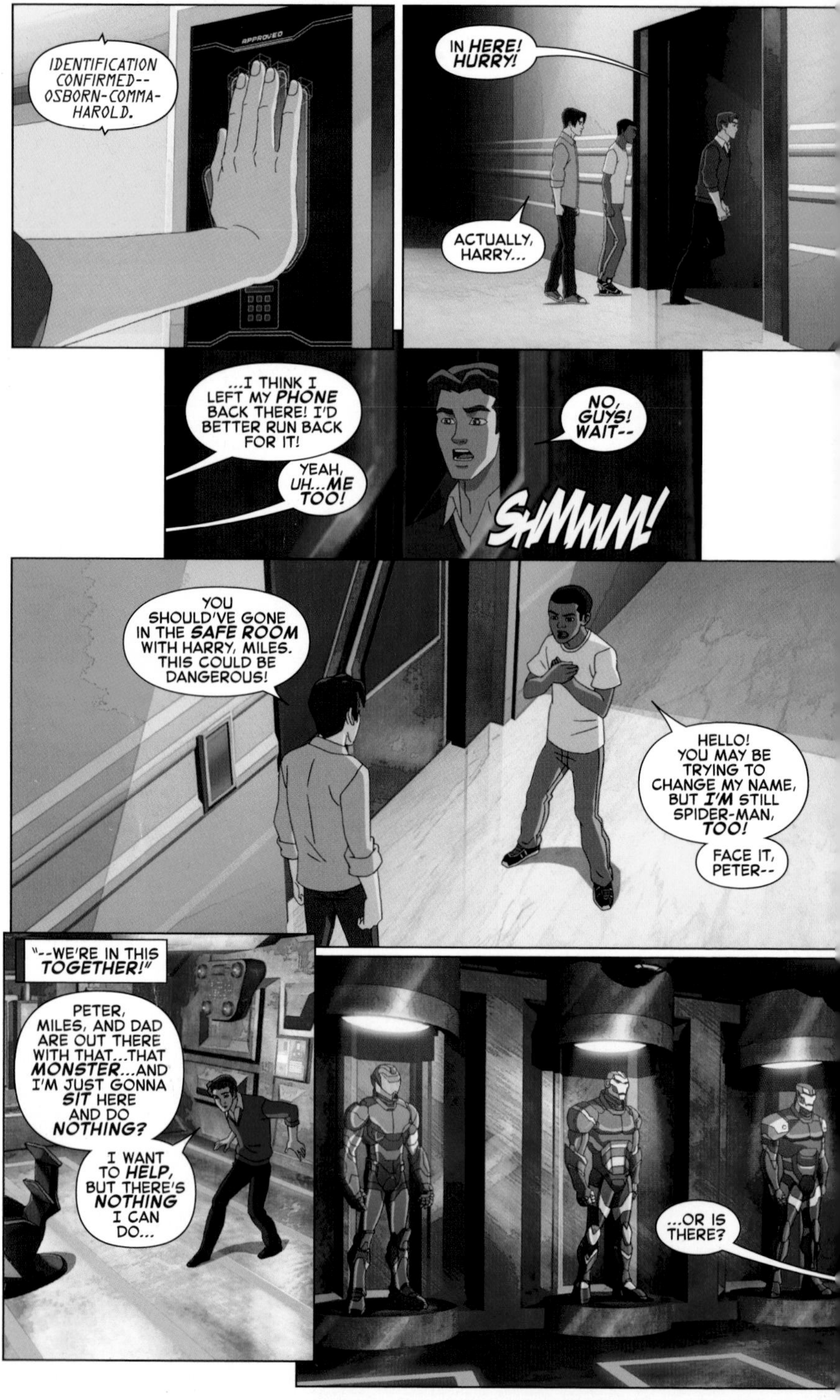

IDENTIFICATION CONFIRMED--OSBORN-COMMA-HAROLD.
APPROVED
IN HERE! HURRY!
ACTUALLY, HARRY...
...I THINK I LEFT MY PHONE BACK THERE! I'D BETTER RUN BACK FOR IT!
YEAH, UH...ME TOO!
NO, GUYS! WAIT--
SHMMM!
YOU SHOULD'VE GONE IN THE SAFE ROOM WITH HARRY, MILES. THIS COULD BE DANGEROUS!
HELLO! YOU MAY BE TRYING TO CHANGE MY NAME, BUT I'M STILL SPIDER-MAN, TOO!
FACE IT, PETER--
"--WE'RE IN THIS TOGETHER!"
PETER, MILES, AND DAD ARE OUT THERE WITH THAT...THAT MONSTER...AND I'M JUST GONNA SIT HERE AND DO NOTHING?
I WANT TO HELP, BUT THERE'S NOTHING I CAN DO...
...OR IS THERE?

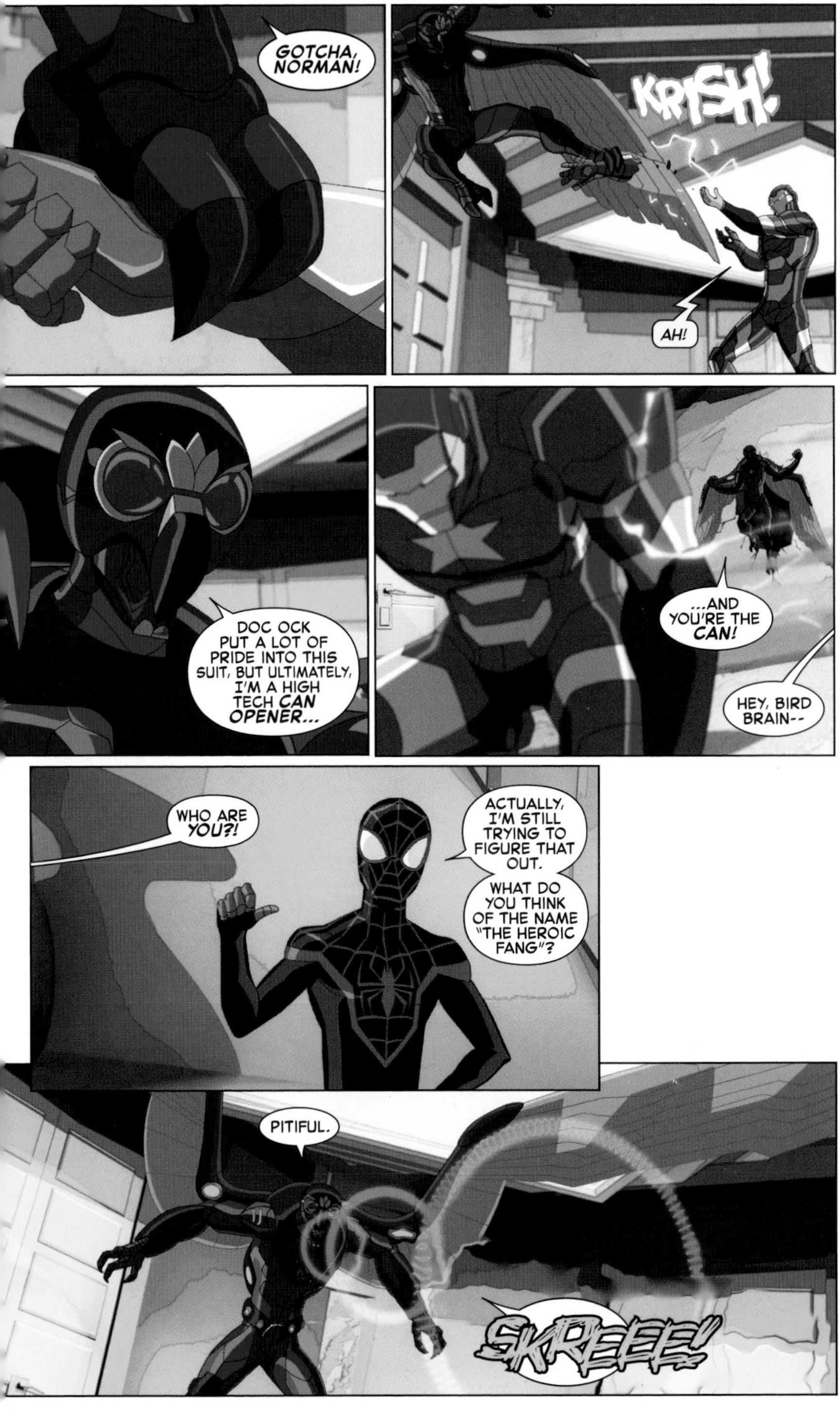
GOTCHA, NORMAN!
KRISH!
AH!
DOC OCK PUT A LOT OF PRIDE INTO THIS SUIT, BUT ULTIMATELY, I'M A HIGH TECH CAN OPENER...
...AND YOU'RE THE CAN!
HEY, BIRD BRAIN--
WHO ARE YOU?!
ACTUALLY, I'M STILL TRYING TO FIGURE THAT OUT.
WHAT DO YOU THINK OF THE NAME "THE HEROIC FANG"?
PITIFUL.
SKREEE!

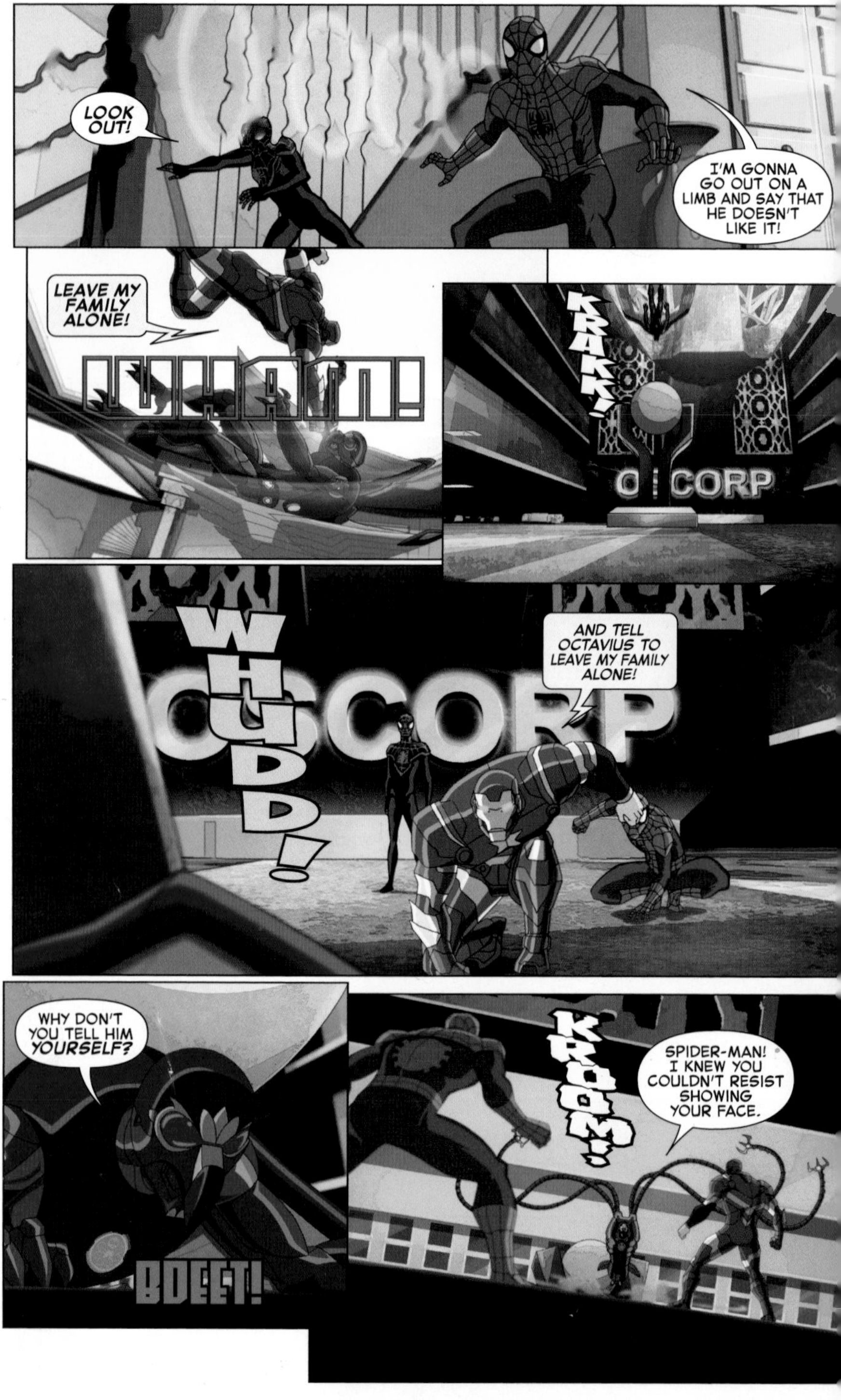
LOOK OUT!
I'M GONNA GO OUT ON A LIMB AND SAY THAT HE DOESN'T LIKE IT!
LEAVE MY FAMILY ALONE!
WHAM!
KRAKK!
OSCORP
WHUDD!
AND TELL OCTAVIUS TO LEAVE MY FAMILY ALONE!
WHY DON'T YOU TELL HIM *YOURSELF?*
BDEET!
KROOM!
SPIDER-MAN! I KNEW YOU COULDN'T RESIST SHOWING YOUR FACE.

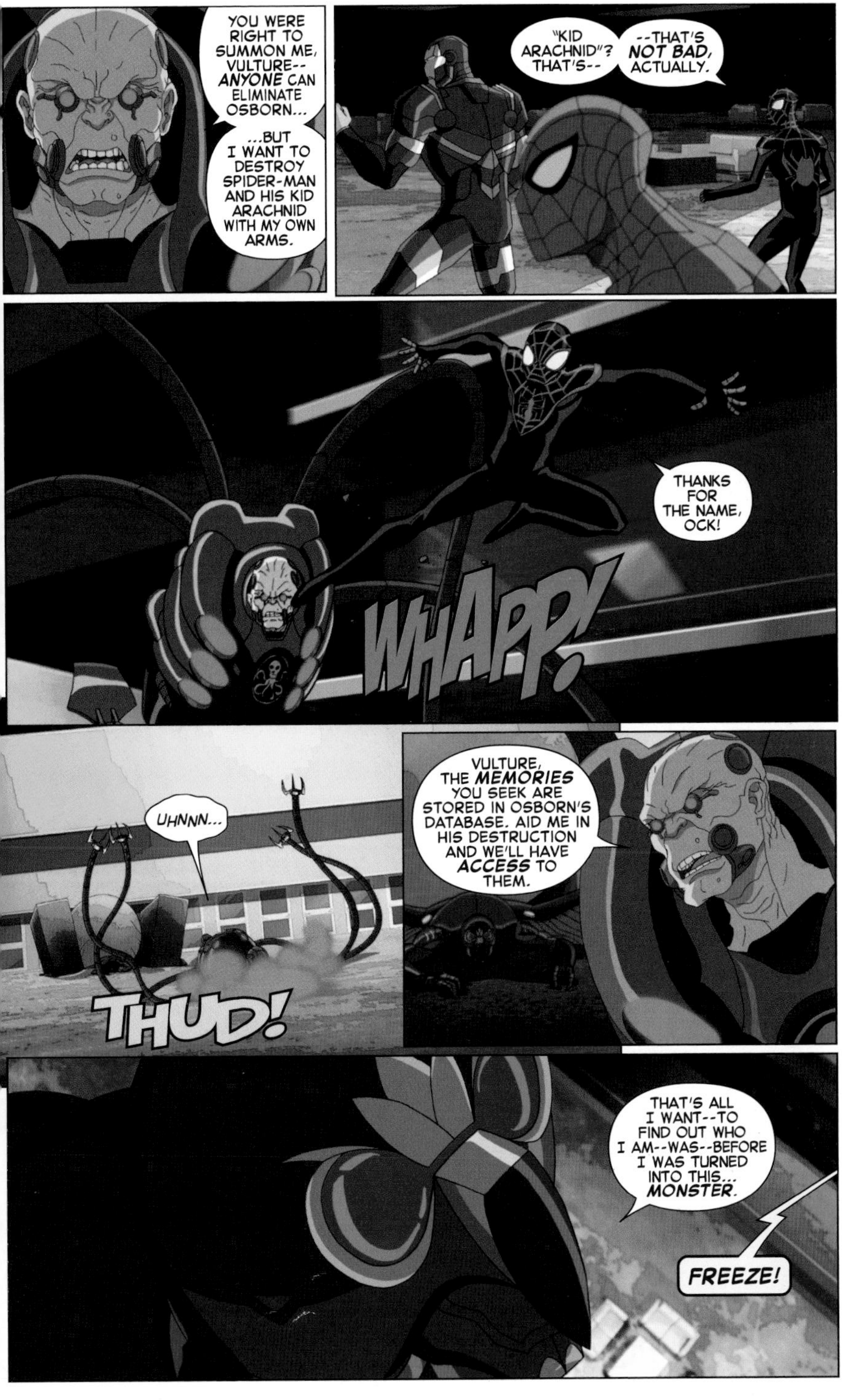
YOU WERE RIGHT TO SUMMON ME, VULTURE-- ANYONE CAN ELIMINATE OSBORN...
...BUT I WANT TO DESTROY SPIDER-MAN AND HIS KID ARACHNID WITH MY OWN ARMS.
"KID ARACHNID"? THAT'S--
--THAT'S NOT BAD, ACTUALLY.
THANKS FOR THE NAME, OCK!
WHAPP!
UHNNN...
THUD!
VULTURE, THE MEMORIES YOU SEEK ARE STORED IN OSBORN'S DATABASE. AID ME IN HIS DESTRUCTION AND WE'LL HAVE ACCESS TO THEM.
THAT'S ALL I WANT--TO FIND OUT WHO I AM--WAS--BEFORE I WAS TURNED INTO THIS... MONSTER.
FREEZE!

N-NOBODY MOVE! OR... OR ELSE!
IS THAT HARRY?
YOU'RE RIGHT--THIS WORLD IS COMPLETELY OFF ITS ROCKER.
LEAVE US ALONE, OCK, OR FACE THE WRATH OF THE PATRIOTEER!
DON'T BE RIDICULOUS, CHILD...
VULTURE, DESTROY HIM!
SKREEE!
WHOA!
SHRAM!

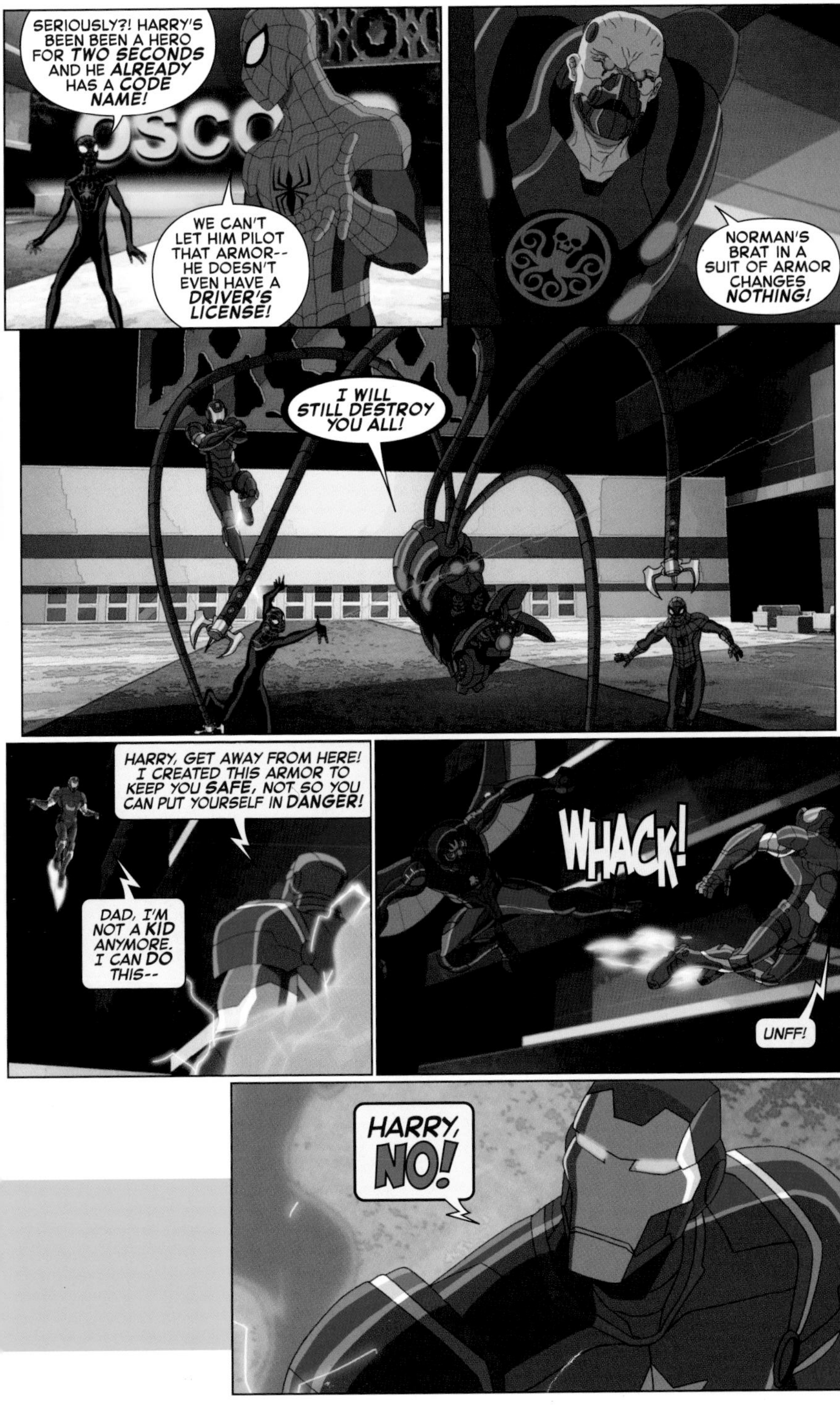
SERIOUSLY?! HARRY'S BEEN BEEN A HERO FOR TWO SECONDS AND HE ALREADY HAS A CODE NAME!
WE CAN'T LET HIM PILOT THAT ARMOR-- HE DOESN'T EVEN HAVE A DRIVER'S LICENSE!
NORMAN'S BRAT IN A SUIT OF ARMOR CHANGES NOTHING!
I WILL STILL DESTROY YOU ALL!
HARRY, GET AWAY FROM HERE! I CREATED THIS ARMOR TO KEEP YOU SAFE, NOT SO YOU CAN PUT YOURSELF IN DANGER!
DAD, I'M NOT A KID ANYMORE. I CAN DO THIS--
WHACK!
UNFF!
HARRY, NO!

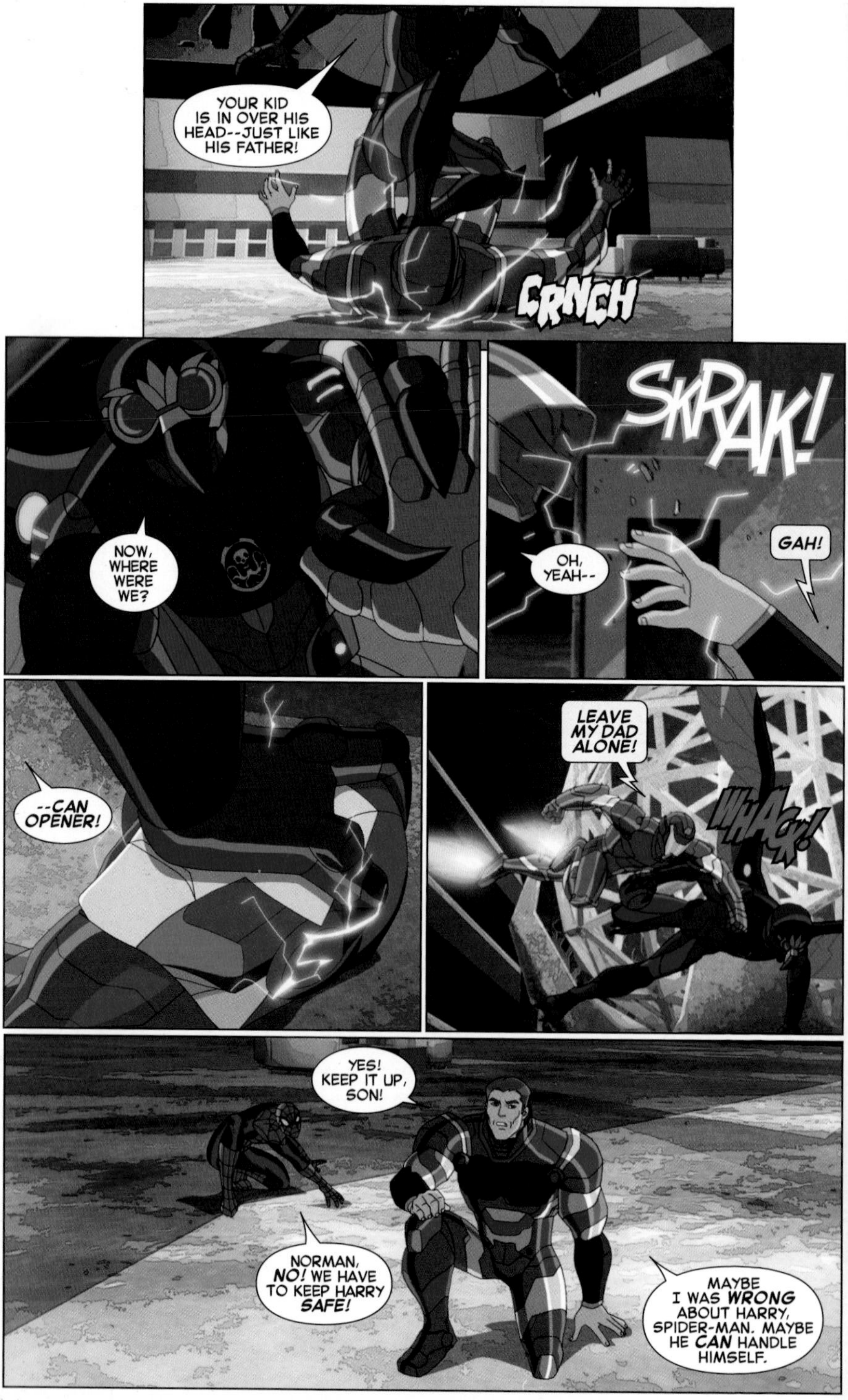
YOUR KID IS IN OVER HIS HEAD--JUST LIKE HIS FATHER!
CRNCH
NOW, WHERE WERE WE?
SKRAK!
OH, YEAH--
GAH!
--CAN OPENER!
LEAVE MY DAD ALONE!
WHACK!
YES! KEEP IT UP, SON!
NORMAN, NO! WE HAVE TO KEEP HARRY SAFE!
MAYBE I WAS WRONG ABOUT HARRY, SPIDER-MAN. MAYBE HE CAN HANDLE HIMSELF.

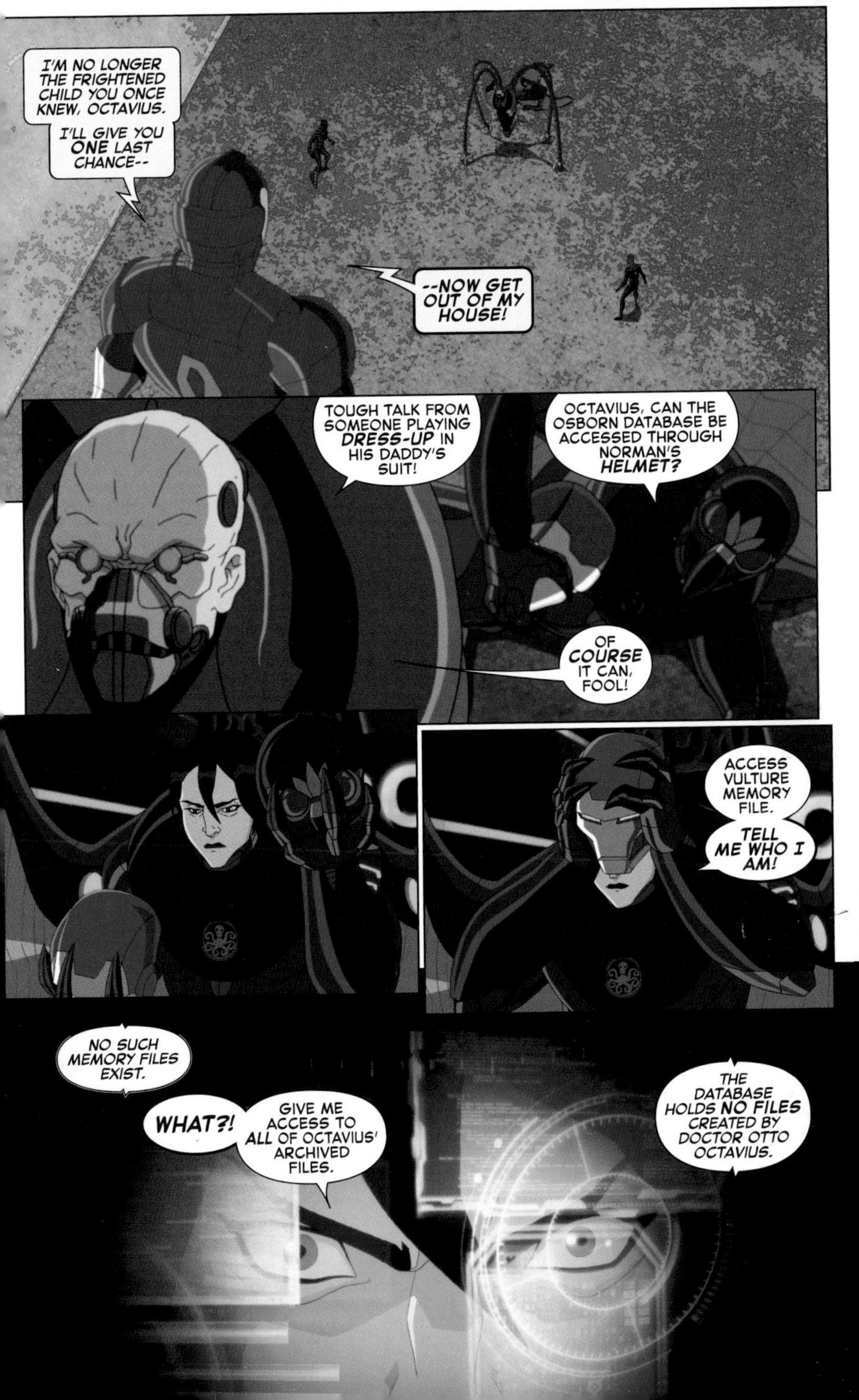
I'M NO LONGER THE FRIGHTENED CHILD YOU ONCE KNEW, OCTAVIUS.
I'LL GIVE YOU ONE LAST CHANCE--
--NOW GET OUT OF MY HOUSE!
TOUGH TALK FROM SOMEONE PLAYING DRESS-UP IN HIS DADDY'S SUIT!
OCTAVIUS, CAN THE OSBORN DATABASE BE ACCESSED THROUGH NORMAN'S HELMET?
OF COURSE IT CAN, FOOL!
ACCESS VULTURE MEMORY FILE.
TELL ME WHO I AM!
NO SUCH MEMORY FILES EXIST.
WHAT?!
GIVE ME ACCESS TO ALL OF OCTAVIUS' ARCHIVED FILES.
THE DATABASE HOLDS NO FILES CREATED BY DOCTOR OTTO OCTAVIUS.

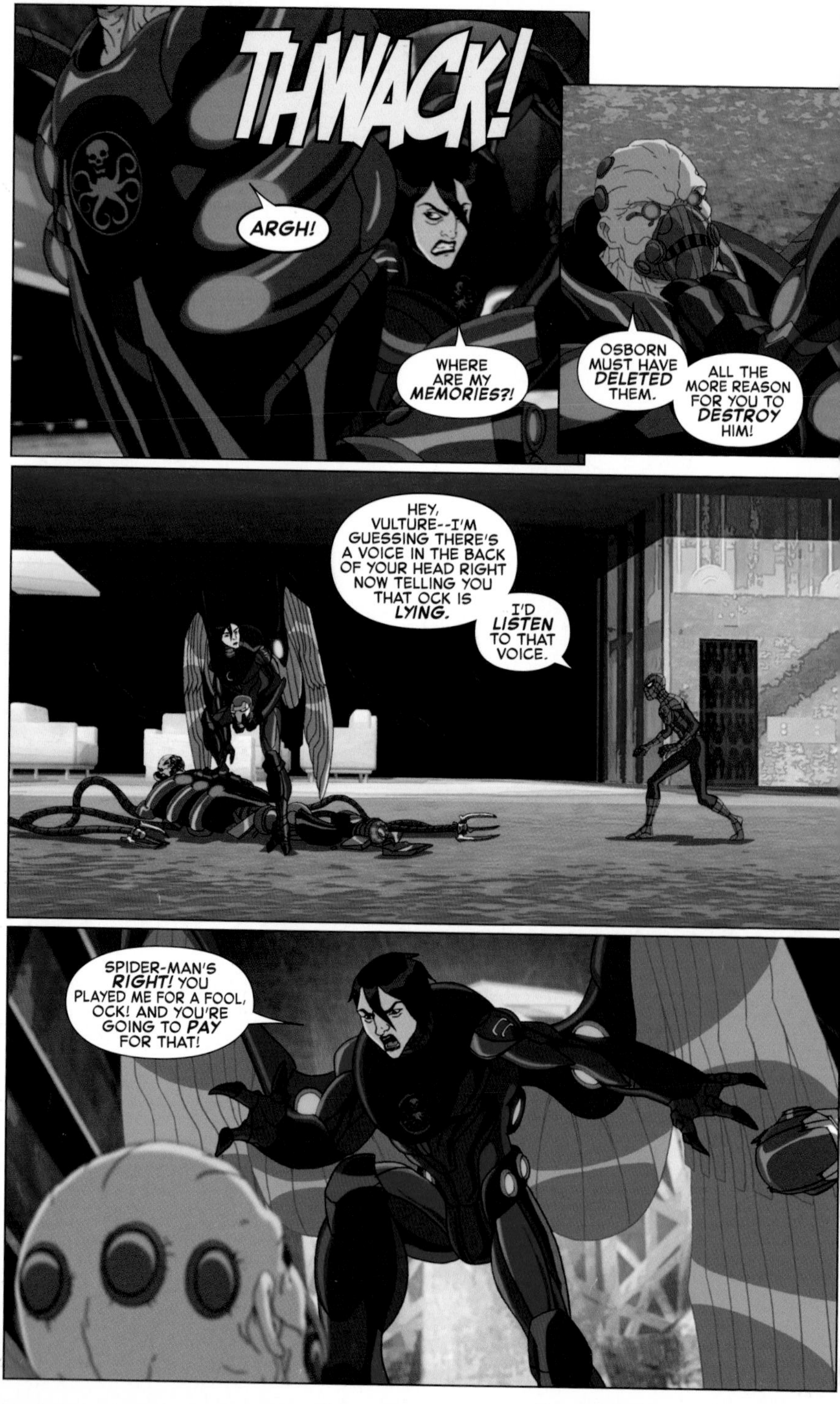
THWACK!
ARGH!
WHERE ARE MY MEMORIES?!
OSBORN MUST HAVE DELETED THEM.
ALL THE MORE REASON FOR YOU TO DESTROY HIM!
HEY, VULTURE--I'M GUESSING THERE'S A VOICE IN THE BACK OF YOUR HEAD RIGHT NOW TELLING YOU THAT OCK IS LYING.
I'D LISTEN TO THAT VOICE.
SPIDER-MAN'S RIGHT! YOU PLAYED ME FOR A FOOL, OCK! AND YOU'RE GOING TO PAY FOR THAT!

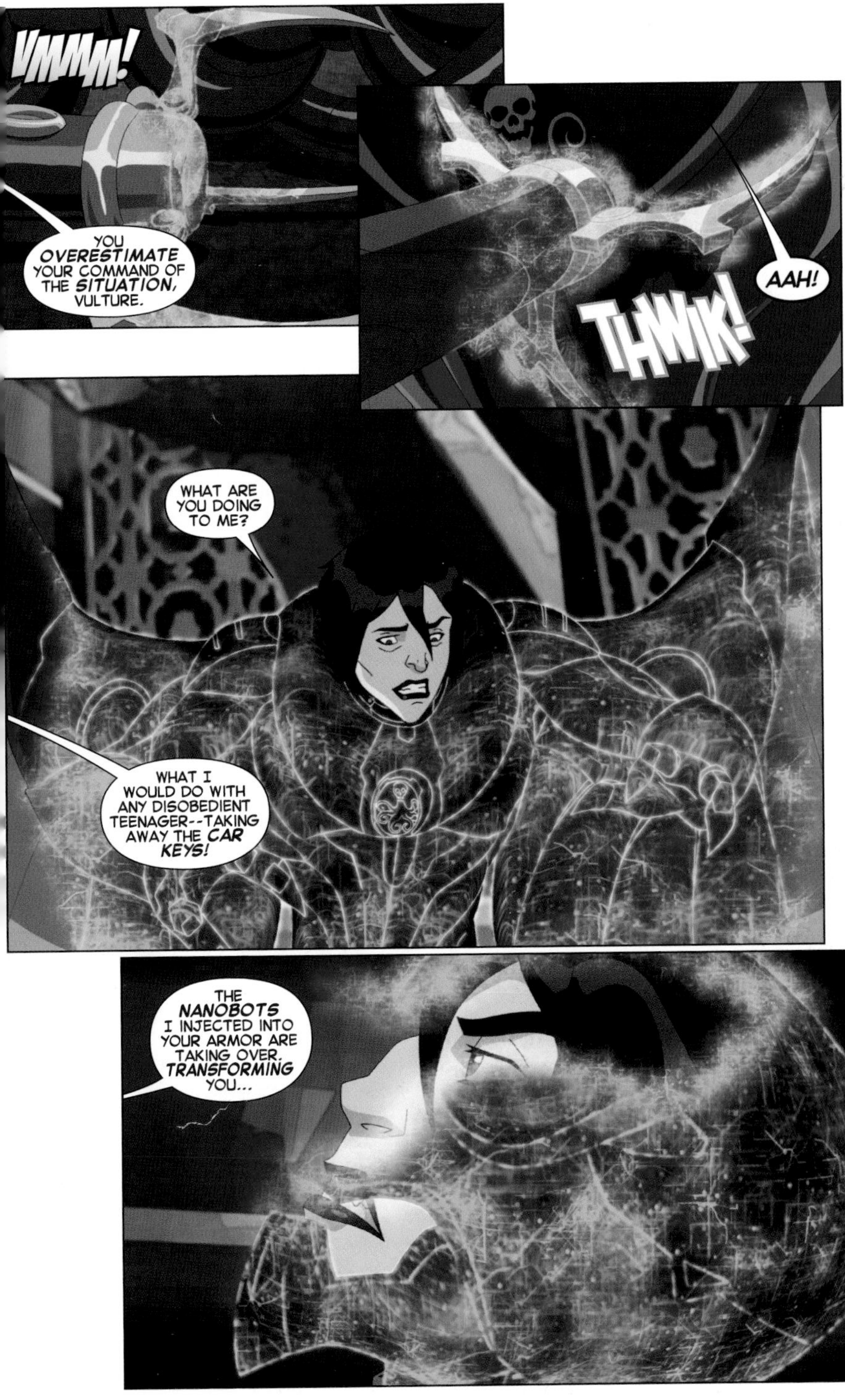
VMMM!
YOU OVERESTIMATE YOUR COMMAND OF THE SITUATION, VULTURE.
AAH!
THWIK!
WHAT ARE YOU DOING TO ME?
WHAT I WOULD DO WITH ANY DISOBEDIENT TEENAGER--TAKING AWAY THE CAR KEYS!
THE NANOBOTS I INJECTED INTO YOUR ARMOR ARE TAKING OVER. TRANSFORMING YOU...

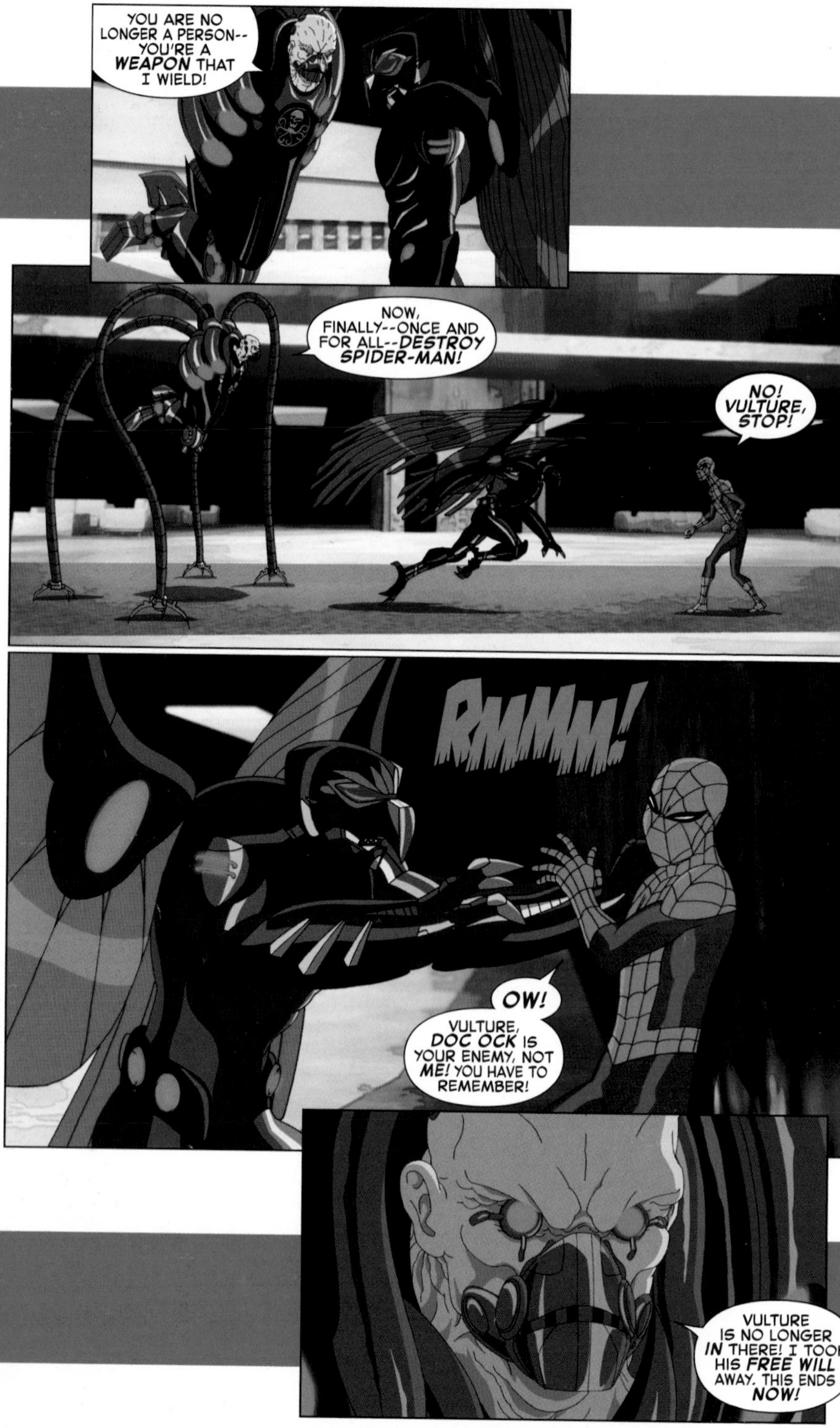

YOU ARE NO LONGER A PERSON-- YOU'RE A *WEAPON* THAT I WIELD!
NOW, FINALLY--ONCE AND FOR ALL--*DESTROY SPIDER-MAN!*
NO! VULTURE, STOP!
RMMM!
OW!
VULTURE, *DOC OCK* IS YOUR ENEMY, NOT *ME!* YOU HAVE TO REMEMBER!
VULTURE IS NO LONGER *IN* THERE! I TOOK HIS *FREE WILL* AWAY. THIS ENDS *NOW!*

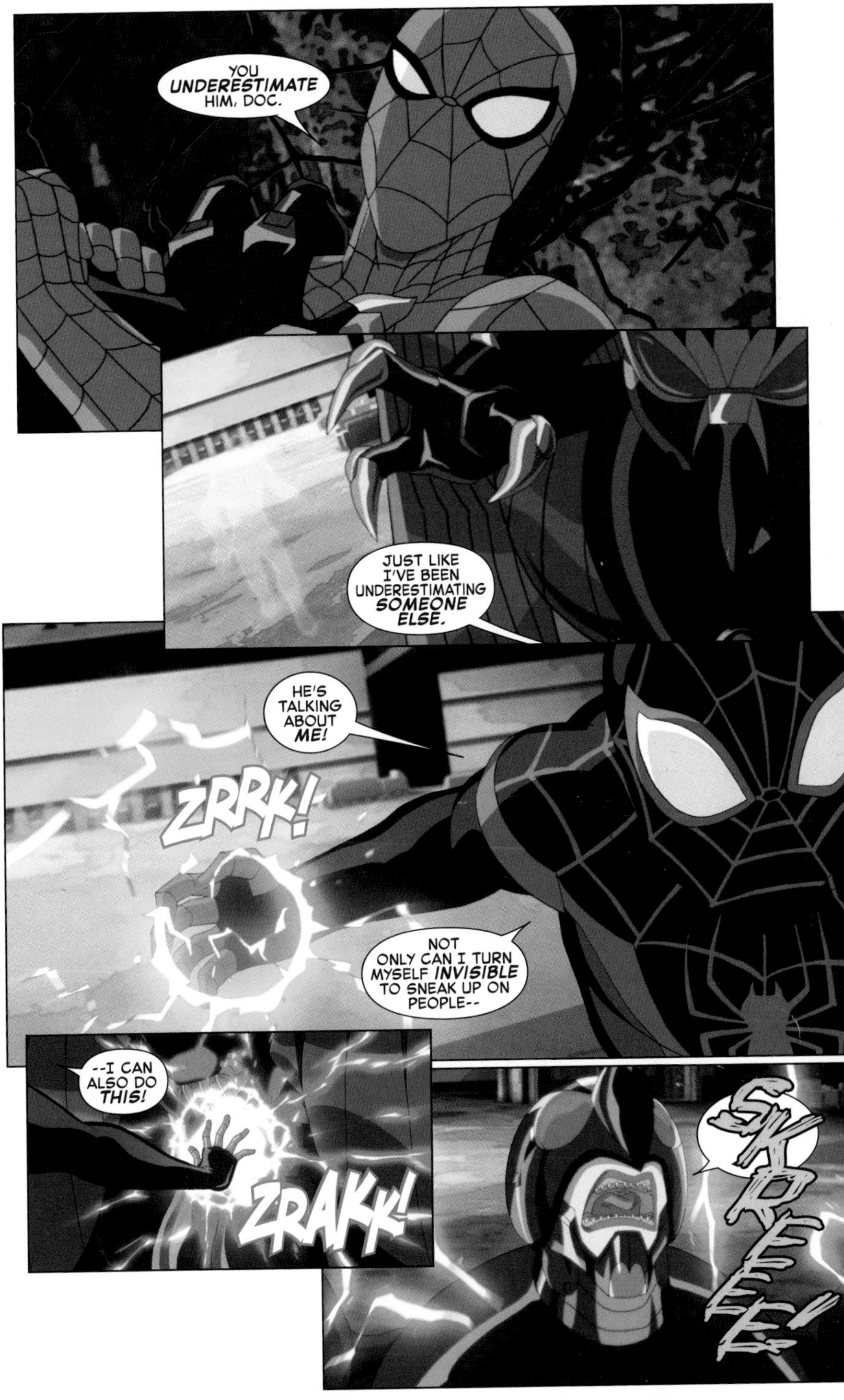
YOU UNDERESTIMATE HIM, DOC.
JUST LIKE I'VE BEEN UNDERESTIMATING SOMEONE ELSE.
HE'S TALKING ABOUT ME!
ZRRK!
NOT ONLY CAN I TURN MYSELF INVISIBLE TO SNEAK UP ON PEOPLE--
--I CAN ALSO DO THIS!
ZRAKK!
SKREEE!

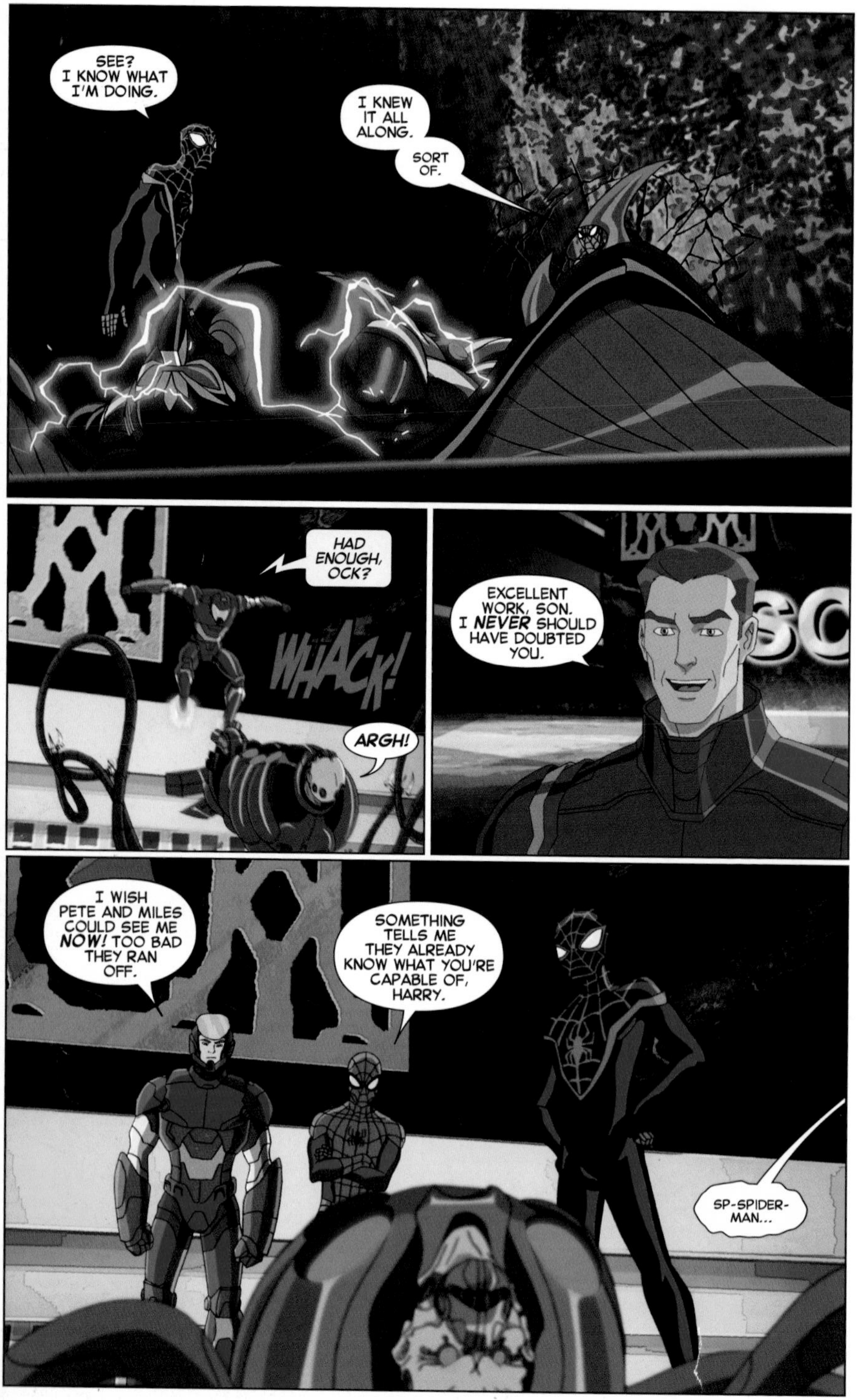
SEE? I KNOW WHAT I'M DOING.
I KNEW IT ALL ALONG.
SORT OF.
HAD ENOUGH, OCK?
WHACK!
ARGH!
EXCELLENT WORK, SON. I NEVER SHOULD HAVE DOUBTED YOU.
I WISH PETE AND MILES COULD SEE ME NOW! TOO BAD THEY RAN OFF.
SOMETHING TELLS ME THEY ALREADY KNOW WHAT YOU'RE CAPABLE OF, HARRY.
SP-SPIDER-MAN...

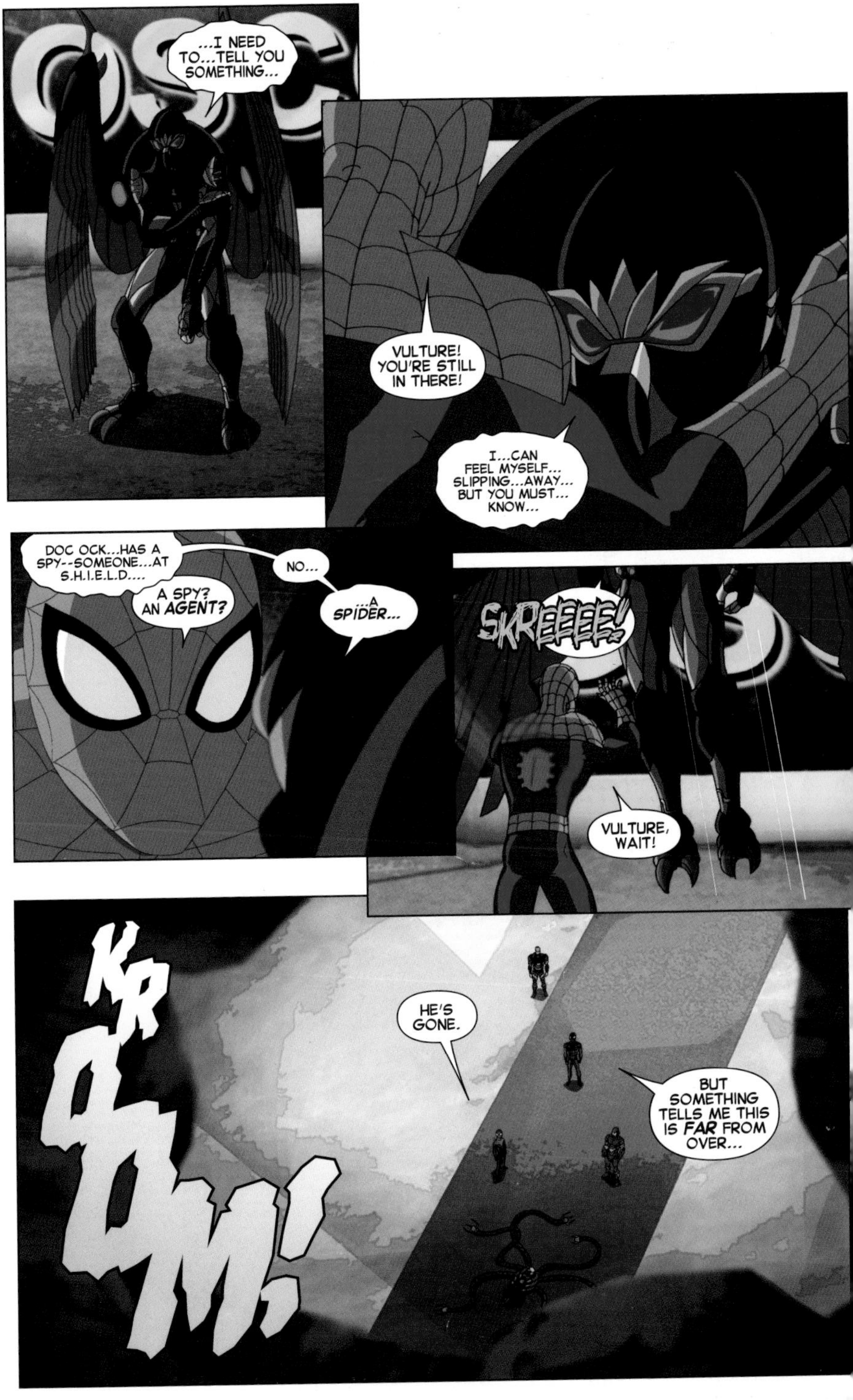
...I NEED TO...TELL YOU SOMETHING...
VULTURE! YOU'RE STILL IN THERE!
I...CAN FEEL MYSELF... SLIPPING...AWAY... BUT YOU MUST... KNOW...
DOC OCK...HAS A SPY--SOMEONE...AT S.H.I.E.L.D....
A SPY? AN AGENT?
NO...
...A SPIDER...
SKREEEE!
VULTURE, WAIT!
KROOM!
HE'S GONE.
BUT SOMETHING TELLS ME THIS IS FAR FROM OVER...

"...EVEN WITH DOCTOR OCTOPUS IN CUSTODY."

THE TRISKELION. S.H.I.E.L.D.'S BASE OF OPERATIONS.

THIS IS BUT A *TEMPORARY* SETBACK FOR MY *GENIUS.*

DO YOU REMEMBER THE *LAST* TIME YOU TRIED TO CONTAIN ME?

SURE. YOU BUSTED THE PLACE UP.

BUT THIS CELL IS BETTER. STRONGER. FACE IT, DOC--

"--YOU'RE STUCK HERE WITH US!"

LISTEN, MILES--I KNOW I'VE BEEN--

OVER-PROTECTIVE? PATRONIZING? I COULD KEEP GOING.

I WAS GOING FOR "ACTING LIKE A BIG BROTHER," BUT I GET THE POINT.

I MIGHT NOT BE AS *EXPERIENCED* A HERO AS YOU ARE, BUT I CAN PROVE THAT I'M *GOOD* AT IT IF YOU'D GIVE ME A CHANCE!

I *KNOW* YOU'RE *GREAT* AT BEING A HERO, IT'S JUST...IT WAS *MY* IDEA TO BRING YOU HERE FROM YOUR WORLD, AND NOW YOU'RE STRANDED ON MINE, AWAY FROM FAMILY AND FRIENDS, I--

I'M JUST TRYING TO GET YOU BACK HOME IN *ONE* PIECE.

MY BEING HERE ISN'T *YOUR* FAULT. I CAME HERE BY CHOICE. I WAS *EAGER* TO JOIN YOU BECAUSE I WANTED TO DO *GOOD.*

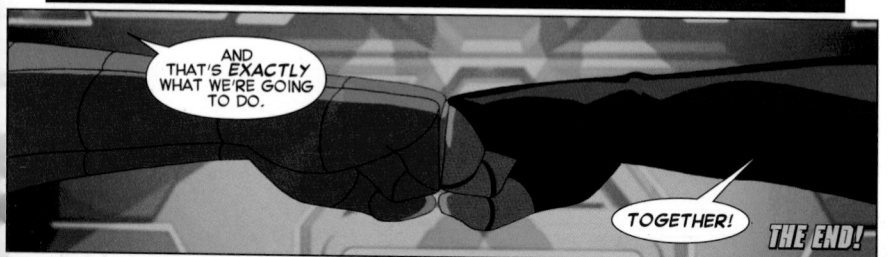

AND THAT'S *EXACTLY* WHAT WE'RE GOING TO DO.

TOGETHER!

THE END!

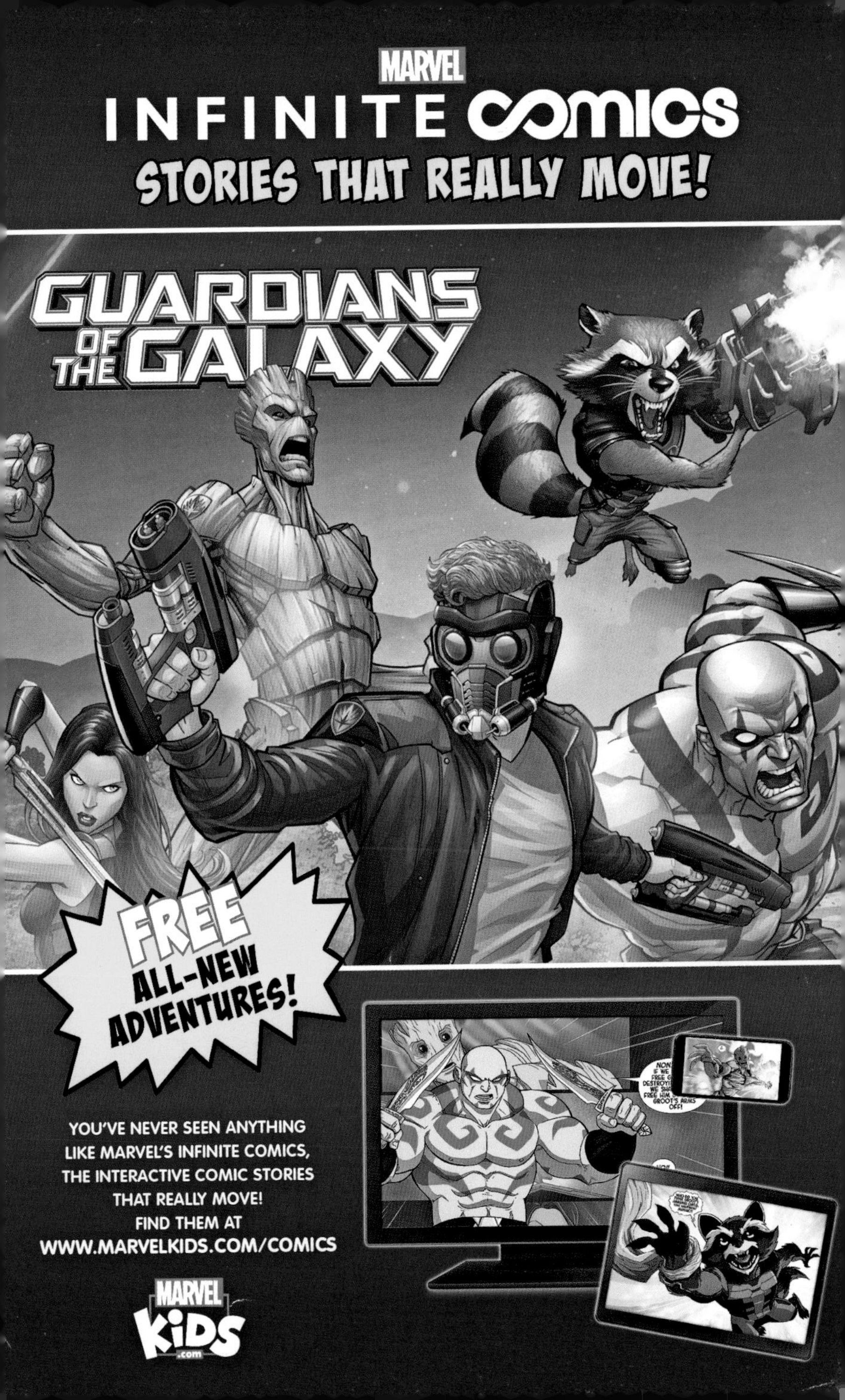
MARVEL
INFINITE COMICS
STORIES THAT REALLY MOVE!
GUARDIANS OF THE GALAXY
FREE ALL-NEW ADVENTURES!
YOU'VE NEVER SEEN ANYTHING LIKE MARVEL'S INFINITE COMICS, THE INTERACTIVE COMIC STORIES THAT REALLY MOVE! FIND THEM AT WWW.MARVELKIDS.COM/COMICS
MARVEL KIDS .com

AVENGERS YOU CAN ASSEMBLE!

LITTLE MARVEL STANDEE PUNCH-OUT BOOK

BY SKOTTIE YOUNG

ISBN: 978-1-302-90202-5
Ages 14 and up

To find a comic shop near you, visit www.comicshoplocator.com or call 1-888-comicbook.

AVAILABLE NOW IN PRINT AND DIGITAL WHEREVER BOOKS ARE SOLD

FEATURING DIE-CUT MARVEL CHARACTERS DRAWN BY *SKOTTIE YOUNG!*

Each standee approximately 3" x 5"

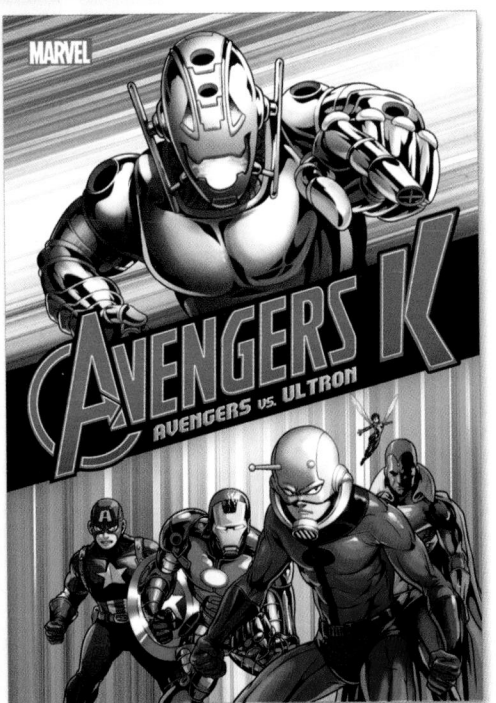

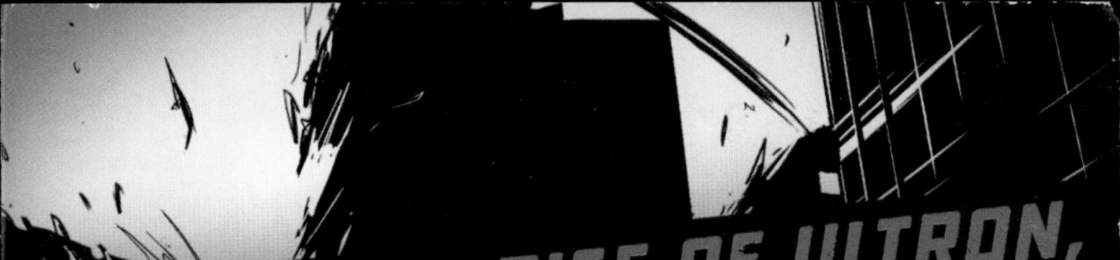

WITNESS THE RISE OF ULTRON, REIMAGINED AND RETOLD IN THRILLING SOUTH KOREAN MANHWA STYLE!

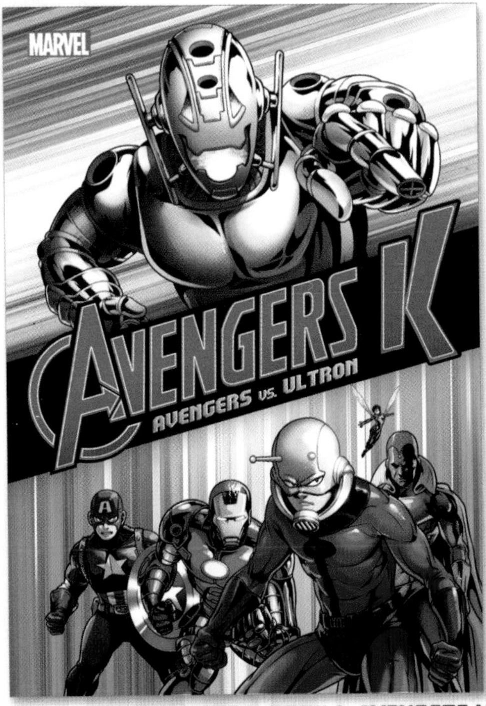

MARVEL
AVENGERS K
AVENGERS VS. ULTRON

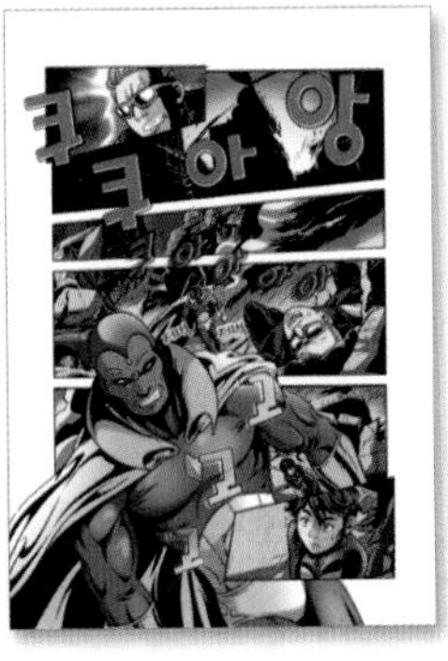

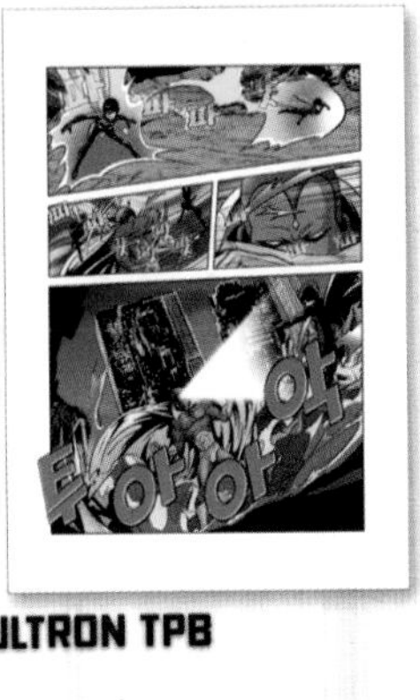

AVENGERS K BOOK 1: AVENGERS VS. ULTRON TPB

ISBN: 978-1-302-90120-2

COLLECTED IN ENGLISH FOR THE FIRST TIME!

AVAILABLE MAY 2016
IN PRINT AND DIGITAL WHEREVER BOOKS ARE SOLD

MARVEL

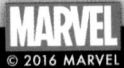

DEADPOOL AND WOLVERINE.
WHAT'S THE WORST THAT CAN HAPPEN?

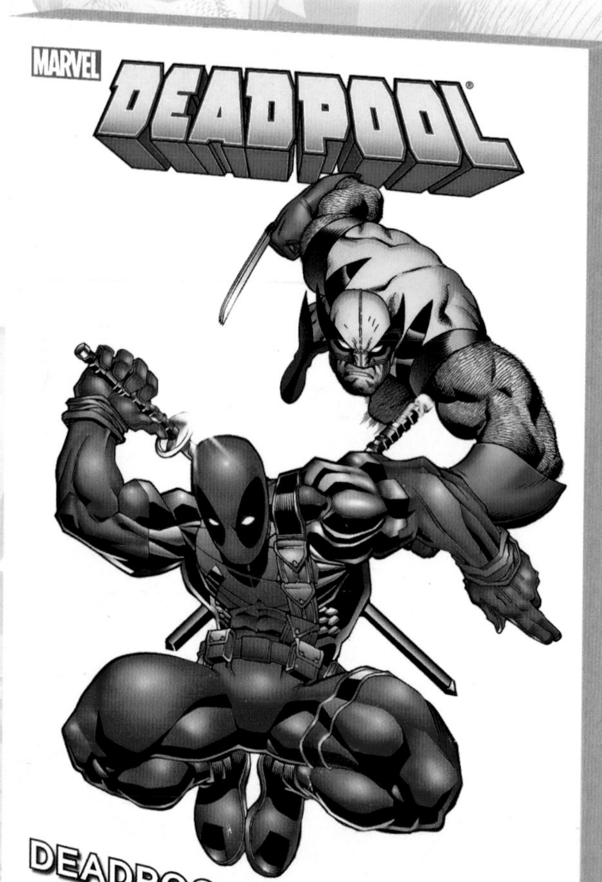

MARVEL UNIVERSE DEADPOOL & WOLVERINE DIGEST
978-1-302-90024-3

ON SALE NOW
IN PRINT AND DIGITAL WHEREVER BOOKS ARE SOLD

TO FIND A COMIC SHOP NEAR YOU, VISIT WWW.COMICSHOPLOCATOR.COM OR CALL 1-888-COMICBOOK

© 2015 Marvel